THE COMPLETE

Letter Writer

To get the results you want

THE COMPLETE

Letter Writer

To get the results you want

foulsham
LONDON • NEW YORK • TORONTO • SYDNEY

foulsham

The Publishing House, Bennetts Close, Cippenham, Slough, Berkshire, SL1 5AP, England

Foulsham books can be found in all good bookshops and direct from www.foulsham.com

ISBN: 978-0-572-03482-5

Copyright © 2008 W. Foulsham

Cover photograph © Superstock

A CIP record for this book is available from the British Library

The moral right of the author has been asserted

All rights reserved

While every effort has been made to ensure the accuracy of all the information contained within this book, neither the author nor the publisher can be liable for any errors. In particular, since laws change from time to time, it is vital that each individual checks relevant legal details for themselves.

Printed in Great Britain by Creative Print & Design, Wales.

Contents

How to use this book

If you have problems with writing letters, you are not alone. The purpose of this book is to help you overcome any issues that cause difficulty. You might not write letters very often, or you might be particularly anxious to make a good impression. Perhaps you are on unfamiliar territory, dealing with sensitive or formal themes. Whatever your individual need, there is sure to be a specimen letter in this book that you can use as a basis for your own.

The first chapter deals with the fundamental aspects of letter writing, and it is worth reading this carefully, especially if you are not very confident. After you have done this, look through the book to find out if there is a letter included that deals exactly with your subject. If there is, you can go ahead and follow the wording given, making whatever alterations are necessary regarding names, addresses, dates and specific details.

If you can't find exactly what you want, there is almost certainly one that deals with something similar. For instance, you might want to write a letter to a person reminding them that they have not paid the rent for a garage that you lease to them. There is no example actually referring to renting a garage, but there are letters regarding the overdue rent for houses and you can base your letter on one of these.

You may also find that you can say what you have in mind more satisfactorily by piecing together passages from different specimen letters. But be careful when doing this to make the parts match up; for example, don't start by saying 'I' and then move on to 'we'.

Later in the book, there is a chapter dealing with e-mail, for which different rules can apply. It is possible to write an e-mail in the same way as you would write a letter, but most people take a rather different approach. E-mail seems surprisingly prone to causing misunderstandings, and tips are also provided for avoiding these.

How to write a letter | 1

A letter is designed to convey information clearly, but the tone and style depend largely on to whom you are writing and why. An application for a job, a complaint about poor service, a love letter, a request for a child to be excused sport – there are so many forms of letter, and they each require a different approach. Nevertheless, they all have some fundamental aspects in common.

First of all, think for a moment about whether writing a letter is the most appropriate form of communication for what you want to achieve. These days, letters can sometimes seem a bit formal, and a telephone call or e-mail might be a better choice. On the other hand, a telephone call or e-mail is generally not suitable for replying to a formal written invitation, sending condolences, expressing your concerns to your MP, and so on.

You should also consider whether to send any form of communication at all! For example, if you are thinking of committing to paper some controversial opinions about something, it may be wise to keep them to yourself – or perhaps to write them down, then think again in a day or two about whether or not to send them.

It has been said that 'the letter you write is you'; so if you want to create a good impression, you need to write the best letter possible. This applies not only to the content, but also to the quality of your handwriting or word processing, the paper that you write it on, the way you address the envelope – and sticking the stamp on neatly and in the right place always helps! These may seem obvious recommendations, but it is all too easy to irritate someone or to give the wrong impression by being a little careless. This book will help you with all these issues.

Stationery

If possible, always choose good-quality notepaper so that the person receiving your letter feels valued and respected.

Paper

Bond paper is designed for letter writing, so this is ideal. It is best to use plain paper for business letters, most often white, although a pale blue or cream is acceptable. Many colours, designs and patterns are available for personal correspondence, and you can pick some to suit your character and those of your recipients.

Sheets of A4 size are best for all but personal correspondence, but A5 (half the size of A4) may be better if the letter is relatively short. The thickness of the paper should be at least $90g/m^2$ but $100g/m^2$ is even better; $80g/m^2$ is only really suitable for photocopies or faxes. Very thin airmail paper is not so much used today, but it does reduce the weight if your letter is several pages long.

Envelopes

In general, the paper and the envelope should match, but an exception may be when several sheets are enclosed in a large envelope. Envelope sizes vary, but the most appropriate for a business letter of no more than one or two sheets of A4 is known as a DL, and will take an A4 letter folded into three parts; you should never fold a letter more than twice. Other envelope sizes are just large enough to take an unfolded letter: C4 for A4 letters, C5 for A5 letters. A C6 envelope will take an A5 letter folded in half, ideal for an informal letter, or an invitation perhaps.

Using postcards

Plain postcards, rather than the picture variety sent from holiday destinations, are not often used these days. Gone are the days when they were cheaper than a letter. They can still provide a handy way of sending messages, and are particularly used for competition entries; it is clearly easier for the people checking the entries if they do not have to open a letter. Other forms of picture postcard, with reproductions of paintings, for example, can be an attractive way to send a thank-you note or some other form of short message.

If you are using an open postcard to send a note, make sure it is quite impersonal. There should be nothing of a private nature in what is written. Your friends will not thank you if intimate details are revealed, even if the only other person reading it is the postman!

Layout and display

It is important that you lay out the letter correctly and clearly so you give a good impression.

If you are handwriting the letter, use blue or black pen and write as clearly and neatly as you can. A handwritten letter is still the most personal and friendly.

Always allow a clear margin around the contents of the letter, rather than writing all the way to the edge of the paper. On an A4 sheet, about 2.5cm (1in) is about right, but use a smaller margin on smaller paper. Use only one side of the paper for a business letter.

Block and indented styles

Most letters are now written or typed in a block style. This means that each new element starts on the left-hand side, flush with the line above. You then leave a line space between paragraphs. This is almost always used for letters written on a word processor or computer.

Alternatively, you can use an indented style, in which case paragraphs are indicated by indenting the first line. There are examples of both styles on pages 13 and 14.

Using word processing

A word processing program is most appropriate for formal letters (and for less formal letters, if you think your handwriting is difficult to read).

Choose a font that is stylish and clear, especially for formal letters, and stick to one font for the whole letter. Among the most popular are Arial, Helvetica, Gill Sans, Trebuchet, Monaco and Times New Roman. Don't be tempted to use a font that imitates handwriting, as it will be difficult to read. Keep eccentric fonts for display on invitations or fun communications; they are not appropriate for letters. The size of the text is important, too. For most letters and fonts, use 12pt.

Use single-space typing for the body of the letter, and leave one line space between the paragraphs. If the letter is very short, you could use double spacing to avoid too much blank space on the paper, but in this case you might be better to use A5 paper instead.

If you find that what you want to write just spills over on to a second page by a few lines, you can reduce the font size slightly, perhaps to 11pt or 10pt but don't make it too small to read easily. Also, some fonts are more economical than others, so you could try changing font to one that uses less space. If these solutions don't work effectively, you may like to change to a more spacious font, or to increase the size so that there is more balance between the two pages.

How to lay out the letter

Two styles of layout are shown here. The first is a personal letter displayed in the indented style, and the second is a business letter in the blocked style.

If the letter is personal, the first thing to write is your address, in full, close to the upper right-hand corner of the page.

If you want to include your telephone number or e-mail address, insert this below the address.

Immediately underneath the address, write the date.

Beneath that, allowing a couple of line spaces, write what is known as the salutation: Dear Mr Smith, Dear Mary.

The main bulk of the letter then follows, broken up into reasonably short paragraphs.

Finally, you sign off with the appropriate closing greeting and sign the letter. Only add your name if your signature is not clear.

25 Milton Street
Andover
Hampshire
AL7 9HJ
24 May 2009

Dear Bill

Thank you so much for your letter. It was lovely to hear from you, especially when I know you are so busy. Your holiday sounded wonderful and I am sure you feel suitably refreshed.

Mary and I would love to take you up on your kind offer of dinner on Saturday 5 June and we look forward to arriving with you at about 8 o'clock.

With kind regards

Roger

Business letters follow a similar pattern, with a few additions. They usually use the blocked style and are sent on headed notepaper. If there is no headed paper, type the business name and address at the top right, as you would for a personal letter.

If you have a reference from the company to quote, this should be typed on the left-hand side above the addressee's details.

Write or type the business name and address of the addressee on the left-hand side of the paper, starting just below the date.

Below the salutation, include a heading, in bold or underlined, to show the subject of the letter.

After the closing greeting, add your own name, and job title, if appropriate, allowing a space for your signature.

If there are any enclosures, indicate this by writing or typing 'Enc' at the bottom of the letter.

Gloucester Bath Products
65 High Street
Gloucester SL6 8HJ

29 June 2009

Mr Ian Smith
Taps and Things
45 Holme Road
Gloucester
GL5 9KL

Dear Mr Smith

Delivery of order 897659

Thank you for your confirmation of the delivery address of this order. The goods are now being packed and will be despatched tomorrow, to arrive with you by 3 July.

I attach the list of items ordered with their code numbers for any future orders.

Thank you for your custom. Please do not hesitate to contact me if you have any queries.

Yours sincerely

Peter Green

Product Manager

Enc

Abbreviations

It is no longer necessary to use full stops after any abbreviated words, especially after abbreviations that end with the final letter of the word, such as Mr, Mrs, Dr or Revd, although this is common in US English. You may find that many people still use a full point after abbreviations that do not end with the final letter of the word, such as Enc.

The address

Include full addresses on your letter and remember the following important points:

- Include the number of the flat or suite of offices, its floor or block, if relevant.
- Use the number of the house, if it has one, and not just the name.
- There is no need to use a comma after the house number.
- The name of a house does not need inverted commas. So, for example, write Pembridge not 'Pembridge'.
- In country districts, include the nearest post town as well as the actual village name.
- Do not use the name of the county town when you mean the county, so don't write Cambridge when you mean Cambridgeshire.
- There is no need to include the county in the address when the letter is going to the county town. For example, when posting to Stafford, there is no need to add Staffordshire to the address. Similarly with the major cities: London, Birmingham, Cardiff and so on.
- Always include the postcode. There is no punctuation before or within the postcode.
- There is no need to include commas at the end of each line of the address or a full stop at the end of the last line.

If you are happy to be contacted by e-mail in response to a letter, you can include your e-mail address after your postal address on a letter.

The date

Every letter should be dated, preferably below the sender's address on the right-hand side.

You can choose from several different formats, the first one here being the most common.

- 5 January 2009
- January 5, 2009
- 5th January 2009
- January 5th, 2009

Abbreviated forms are best kept for informal letters. The full stop after abbreviations such as Jan is now rarely used. The use of the comma in any style of date is also dwindling. Abbreviating the date to all numbers, such as 5.1.09, can be confusing because Americans put the month before the day. In this case, they would read the date as May 1, not 5 January.

- 5 Jan, 2009
- Jan 5, 2009
- Jan 5th, 2009
- 5th Jan 2009
- 5:1:09
- 5.1.09
- 5/1/09

Forms of address

These are fairly straightforward, and you should only ensure that you set the right level of familiarity. Do not address someone as 'Dear Bill', for example, when it is more appropriate to address the letter to 'Mr W. Brown' and use the opening 'Dear Mr Brown'.

- Use Mr, Mrs, Miss or Ms, as appropriate. If you do not know whether a woman prefers to be called Miss or Mrs, then use Ms.
- Never use the outdated form of addressing a woman by her husband's name, for example 'Mrs Roger Smith'.
- Esq is short for Esquire but is always abbreviated. It is an alternative to Mr so you should never use both together. It is rarely used today.
- Messrs is used for letters to a firm the name of which incorporates individual surnames, although it is rarely used these days.

Writing to titled people

When writing to titled people, it is courteous to use the correct form of address. Below is a list of titles and offices giving the correct way to:

1 Address the envelope
2 Start the letter
3 Close the letter

The Queen

1 Her Most Gracious Majesty Queen Elizabeth II
2 Madam OR May it please your Majesty
3 I have the honour to remain your Majesty's most faithful servant

However, it is more likely that you will write via her private secretary, and the letter should be addressed to him or her at Buckingham Palace, beginning the letter 'Dear Sir' or 'Dear Madam' and ending 'Yours faithfully'.

Royal Princes, Royal Dukes

1 His Royal Highness (then give title, such as the Prince of Wales)
2 Sir OR Your Royal Highness
3 I have the honour to remain, Sir, your Royal Highness's most dutiful servant

Royal Princesses, Royal Duchesses

1 Her Royal Highness (then give title, such as the Princess Royal)
2 Madam OR Your Royal Highness
3 I have the honour to remain, Madam, your Royal Highness's most dutiful servant

Other Princes and Princesses

1 Her Highness (then give title)
2 Madam OR Your Highness
3 I have the honour to remain, Madam, your Royal Highness's dutiful servant

Dukes

1 His Grace the Duke of *place*
2 My Lord Duke OR Dear Duke
3 I remain, my Lord Duke, your Grace's most obedient servant

Duchess

1 Her Grace the Duchess of *place*
2 Madam OR Dear Duchess
3 I remain, Madam, your Grace's most obedient servant

Marquess

1 The Most Honourable the Marquess of *place*
2 My Lord Marquess OR Dear Lord *name*
3 I remain, my Lord Marquess, your Lordship's most obedient servant

Marchioness

1 The Most Honourable the Marchioness of *place*
2 Madam OR Dear Lady *name*
3 I remain, Madam, your Ladyship's most obedient servant

Earl

1 The Right Honourable the Earl of *place*
2 My Lord OR Dear Lord *name*
3 I remain, my Lord, your Lordship's most obedient servant

Countess

1 The Right Honourable the Countess of *place*
2 Madam OR Dear Lady *name*
3 I remain, Madam, your Ladyship's most obedient servant

Viscount

1 The Right Honourable the Lord Viscount *name*
2 My Lord OR Dear Lord *name*
3 I remain, my Lord, your Lordship's most obedient servant

Viscountess

1 The Right Honourable the Lady Viscountess *name*
2 Madam OR Dear Lady *name*
3 I remain, Madam, your Ladyship's most obedient servant

Baron

1 The Right Honourable Lord *name*
2 My Lord OR Dear Lord *name*
3 I remain, my Lord, your Lordship's most obedient servant

Baroness
1   The Right Honourable Lady *name*
2   Madam OR Dear Lady *name*
3   I remain, Madam, your Ladyship's most obedient servant

Baronet
1   Sir *first and surname*, Bt (not Bart)
2   Sir
3   No special form

Baronet's wife
1   Lady *surname only*, unless born with a title in her own right
2   Madam OR Dear Lady *surname*
3   No special form

Dame
1   Dame *forename and surname*
2   Dear Dame *forename*
3   No special form

Knight
1   Sir *forename and surname*
2   Dear Sir *forename*
3   No special form

Wife of knight
1   Lady s*urname only*, unless born with a title in her own right
2   Madam OR Dear Lady *surname*
3   No special form

Writing to members of the government
The Prime Minister
1   The Rt Hon *forename and surname* MP
2   Dear Prime Minister
3   No special form

The Chancellor of the Exchequer
1   The Rt Hon *forename and surname* MP
2   Dear Chancellor
3   No special form

Secretaries of State and other ministers

1 As for Prime Minister, or by appointment, for example, The Foreign Secretary or The Secretary of State for Education
2 By appointment, such as Dear Secretary of State, Dear Foreign Secretary, Dear Minister, etc.
3 No special form

Writing to people in diplomatic posts

The following are for British representatives, and each may have other titles and qualifications that it may be appropriate to add. For representatives of foreign countries, a telephone call to the embassy concerned is the quickest way of finding out the correct form.

British Ambassadors

1 His Excellency HBM's Ambassador and Plenipotentiary to the Court of *whoever*
2 Dear *name and title* OR Dear Ambassador OR (very formally) Your Excellency
3 According to rank OR Yours sincerely and respectfully

Governor General

1 His Excellency *name*, Governor General of *place*
2 and 3 According to rank

Governor of Colony

1 His Excellency *name*, Governor of *place*
2 and 3 According to rank

British Consul

1 Mr, Mrs, Miss or Ms *Name*, HBM's Agent and Consul (OR Vice Consul, OR Consul General, as case may be)
2 and 3 No special form

Writing to legal dignitaries

The Lord Chief Justice of England

1 The Rt Hon, The Lord Chief Justice of England, PC
2 Dear Lord Chief Justice
3 No special form

The Lord Justice-General of Scotland
1 The Rt Hon, The Lord Justice-General of Scotland, PC
2 Dear Justice-General
3 No special form

The Master of the Rolls
1 The Master of the Rolls
2 Dear Master of the Rolls
3 No special form

High Court judges
1 The Hon Mr/Mrs Justice *surname*
2 Dear Judge/Madam

Writing to local government officials
Lord Mayor/Lady Mayoress
1 The Right Worshipful the Lord Mayor/Lady Mayoress of *place* EXCEPT FOR the cities of London, York, Belfast and Cardiff, for which the correct form is The Rt Hon The Lord Mayor of *place*
2 Mr Lord Mayor/My Lady Mayoress (formal) OR Dear Lord Mayor/Dear Lady Mayoress (social matters)
3 No special form

Mayors/Mayoresses
1 The Right Worshipful the Mayor/Mayoress of *place*
2 Dear Sir/Madam
3 No special form

Councillors
1 Councillor *forename and surname*
2 Dear Councillor
3 No special form

Writing to members of the clergy
Church of England archbishops
1 The Most Reverend and Rt Hon the Lord Archbishop of *place*
2 Dear Archbishop
3 No special form

Church of England bishops
1 The Right Reverend the Lord Bishop of *place*
2 Dear Bishop
3 No special form

Church of England deans
1 The Very Reverend the Dean of *place*
2 Dear Dean
3 No special form

Church of England archdeacons
1 The Venerable the Archdeacon of *place*
2 Dear Archdeacon
3 No special form

Church of England vicars and rectors
1 Mr/Mrs/Ms or Father
2 Dear Mr/Mrs/Ms *surname* or Father *surname* (it is advisable to find out how they like to be addressed)
3 No special form

Roman Catholic cardinals
1 His Eminence the Cardinal Archbishop of *place* or (if not an Archbishop) His Eminence Cardinal *surname*
2 Dear Cardinal *surname*
3 No special form

Roman Catholic archbishops
1 His Grace the Archbishop of *place*
2 Your Grace OR Dear Archbishop *surname*
3 No special form

Roman Catholic bishops
1 The Right Reverend *forename and surname*, Bishop of *place*
2 My Lord Bishop OR Dear Bishop *surname*
3 No special form

Roman Catholic monsignors
1 The Reverend Monsignor *surname*
2 Dear Monsignor *surname*
3 No special form

Roman Catholic priests
1 Father *surname*
2 Dear Father *surname*
3 No special form

The Chief Rabbi
1 The Chief Rabbi Dr *forename and surname*
2 Dear Chief Rabbi
3 No special form

Rabbis
1 Rabbi *forename and surname*
2 Dear Rabbi *surname*
3 No special form

Imams
1 Imam *forename and surname*
2 Dear Imam
3 No special form

The salutation

This is how you address the recipient of the letter. The following examples should cover most of your letters. For intimate letters, you will have your own forms of address.

Dear Sir Dear Madam Dear Sir or Madam	For business letters if you do not know the name of the recipient. You can use simply Sir or Madam, but they are rather abrupt.
Dear Sirs	For business letters addressed to Messrs So and So or a company name.
Dear Mr Armstrong Dear Mrs Brown Dear Ms Patel Dear Miss Dobrowska	All these are correct when a less formal approach is required.
Dear Alfred Constable Dear Astrid Marker	This form is becoming more common, and suggests a wish for a less formal but nevertheless professional approach to business.
Dear Tom Dear Alice	These are used for business letters if you have a good relationship with the person you are dealing with, and for personal letters.

Opening greetings

The opening sentence of your letter will probably be the hardest to compose, but once you have managed to make a beginning, the subsequent passages will follow more easily.

Business letters often begin by referring to previous correspondence, 'I acknowledge receipt of your letter of *date* and in reply...'. By using this approach, it is easy to link to the main purpose of your letter, which is to respond in some way to the person's letter to you.

Phrases for beginning letters

Any of these phrases may give you an idea of how to open your letter, or you can look through the specimen letters in this book; there should be many that will suit your purpose.

- Following our meeting/telephone conversation of
- I acknowledge your letter of
- I am anxious to hear from you about
- I am pleased to confirm receipt of your letter of
- I am sorry to have to say that
- I find it necessary to
- I greatly appreciate your
- I have carefully considered your
- I have to tell you that
- I hope you received my letter of *date* about *subject*
- I must thank you for
- I recently heard about your sad loss
- I refer to your letter of
- I regret to inform you that
- I wonder if you could
- In accordance with your request
- In reply to your letter of
- It is so long since you wrote that
- It is with considerable pleasure/regret that I
- It was very good of you to
- Many thanks for the beautiful
- Many thanks for your letter of

- Please accept my thanks for
- Please find enclosed
- Recently we had occasion to write to you about
- Thank you for your letter of
- We wish to remind you that
- With reference to your letter of
- You may be interested to hear that
- You may remember that we met at
- You will be sorry, I know, to hear that
- Your letter gave me

Composing the letter

Unless you are a confident letter writer, the best rule to remember is to keep it simple and straightforward. You should try to match the style of the letter to the person you are writing to. If you keep the purpose of the letter and the recipient in mind as you are writing, then you will compose a more satisfactory letter.

Sticking to the subject

Having plunged in, get to the real meat at once. Say what you have to say clearly and briefly, especially if it is a letter trying to get something done or to pass on specific information. Don't waffle or your main message might be overlooked. Even in a personal letter, match the level of detail you include to the recipient. After all, you want to continue the friendship, and the last thing you should do is sound boring.

Use clear language

Don't use involved sentences that seem clumsy or may have two or more meanings. Use straightforward language and only ever use words you fully understand. If you are trying hard to impress, it may seem to be a good idea to embellish your writing with some well-chosen 'big' words. You may use a thesaurus to replace everyday language with something more complex or to avoid using the same word twice. However, unless you are completely confident that you truly understand the words you have chosen, this is a very dangerous practice. If you try to sound clever by using long words when simple ones will do, you are more likely to sound foolish than learned. It is much better to use language with which you are comfortable.

Try not to use hackneyed phrases or clichés in letters, particularly formal ones. This does not give a good impression because it may appear that you have not thought carefully about the letter. If you are worried about copying a particular letter in this book almost word for word, rest assured that each letter has been carefully constructed to seem fresh and distinctive.

In formal letters, try to use correct grammar to ensure that you are taken seriously. If your grammar is shaky, there are some tips on pages 259–283, but that is another reason to keep your text simple and clear; that way you cannot go far wrong. Informal letters can be looser and more colloquial, and letters to really close friends can, of course, contain all kinds of phraseology that other people may find incomprehensible, such as private in-jokes.

Do check your spelling. Spellcheck programs are very useful but not foolproof, as this salutary verse shows.

Eye have a spelling chequer; it came with my pea sea.
It plane lee marks four my revue Miss steaks aye can knot see.
Eye ran this poem threw it, and you'll bee glad two no.
Its very polished in its weigh – my checker tolled me sew.

Make sure the sentences flow logically, especially if you are using sections from a mix of sample letters.

If you have come across the now rarely used Latin abbreviations such as 'ult' (*ultimo mense*, last month), 'inst' (*instante mense*, this month) and 'prox' (*proximo mense*, next month), leave them where you found them! They are old-fashioned and just look silly. Simply use the actual name of the month.

Courtesy

All your letters should be polite and courteous. Whatever the tone of your letter, frame your remarks carefully. Receiving a letter obviously written in haste and being told that the writer was 'in a terrific hurry' or 'extremely busy' is not impressive. What we are really being told is that they begrudge the time that is being wasted on writing to us! At the other end of the spectrum is sycophancy. Nobody is fooled by over-the-top, gushing remarks that clearly lack sincerity.

Even in a personal letter, be careful of repeating gossip. Words have more power when written than spoken and, by definition, the gossip you have heard could be wrong.

Unpleasant letters

If you are writing a letter of complaint, it is important to remain polite and always to avoid stooping to insults or, worse still, libellous statements.

First of all, think carefully about whether to write the letter at all. Sometimes unpleasant things have to be dealt with, but don't write angrily just to let off steam because it could backfire. If you do have anything unpleasant to say, state the facts clearly and avoid insults or exaggeration.

Once you have finished the letter, do not post it immediately. Leave it a day or two, if possible, then read it again. You may decide to throw it away, soften the tone or make some amendments before you send it.

E-mail tone and style

At this stage, it is worth mentioning that although many people use e-mail in a similar way to letters, e-mails are often much shorter, and can, for the sake of clarity, include excerpts from the e-mail to which you are replying. It is quite common for e-mail correspondence to be replied to almost immediately, and the brief comments in each of the messages that pass to and fro may amount to something like a conversation. As a consequence, e-mails often use speech forms and abbreviations.

The immediacy of e-mail also has its drawbacks, however. Misunderstandings can occur if messages are badly worded, and this can lead to the unfortunate response of 'flaming', which means sending an abusive reply without thinking carefully before you do it. Once an e-mail is sent, you cannot stop it reaching its destination, whereas with a letter, at least you have some time for reconsideration before you post it. For more detail, see pages 247–258.

How to close

You should use an appropriate closure to your letter, depending on to whom you are sending it and how formal it is. Obviously, for personal letters, you may have your own greetings.

Yours faithfully	For business letters starting 'Dear Sir' or 'Dear Madam'.
Yours sincerely	For business letters addressed to an individual, such as 'Dear Mr Jones', 'Dear Ms Patel', 'Dear Bill'.
Yours truly	For business letters when something a little more friendly than 'Yours faithfully' is required, although now rather old-fashioned.
With kind regards	Suitable for most business and personal letters.
Best wishes	Used in less formal business letters and at the end of business e-mails.
Love	The most common sign-off for personal letters.

Your signature

Never conclude any letter without signing your name. In a business letter, follow your signature with your printed name, as outlined on page 14. That way it does not matter if your signature is illegible. Depending on how well you know the recipient, you can sign simply your forename, your first and surname, or your initials and surname.

Addressing and sending your letter

First impressions are very important when sending a letter, and the first thing that a recipient will notice is the address on the envelope. If it is well written, the impression will be a good one, but if the wording is badly arranged, there are misspelled words, or the person's title is incorrect, it will certainly be less favourable.

Writing the envelope

If your envelope is clearly addressed, it is more likely to be speedily delivered, so check the notes on addresses on page 15.

To space the wording properly on the envelope, imagine a horizontal line cutting the envelope into two. Start writing the name slightly below the imaginary line. If your handwriting is large and the address is rather long, begin on the imaginary line, or even a little higher. Start writing slightly in from the left-hand edge. Below the name, set out the address in two, three or more lines, as necessary. Match the block or indented style you have used for the letter. If you have chosen an indented style, start each line a little further right than the one above, or, if you prefer a block style, begin each fresh line level with the line above.

Miss Janet Smith
44 Home Hill
Southbridge
Lincolnshire
PE8 6HU

Miss Janet Smith
44 Home Hill
Southbridge
Lincolnshire
PE8 6HU

If you are using a word processing program to address the envelope, try to get the name and address central between the top and bottom of the envelope, and slightly to the left on a long envelope or central on smaller envelopes. Blocked text for a typed address always looks best. Use the preview function on the computer to make sure you feed the envelope into the printer the right way so the address is correctly positioned.

If you are using a window envelope, fold the letter with the writing outside so that the address shows through the transparency.

Before you seal the envelope

Before putting the letter in the envelope, make sure that the recipient's name and initials are given correctly. Check the letter through one last time to ensure that there are no errors. If you have said that you are enclosing something with your letter, make sure you have done so. It is annoying to receive a letter without a promised enclosure.

Fold the letter neatly and evenly two or three times, according to the size of the envelope, then seal up the letter.

Postage

Fix the stamp in the upper right-hand corner, making sure that it is straight and that you have paid the correct amount.

The main options are first and second class mail, the rates for which vary according to the weight and size of the letter. Royal Mail aims to deliver first class mail the following day, and second class mail within three working days.

Secure mail

If your letter is particularly urgent and/or contains something of value, send it Special Delivery, which guarantees delivery by a certain time the next working day. The letter and contents are also insured up to a certain value, and you can choose to pay more for higher levels of compensation in the event that the letter does go astray. A third option is Recorded Delivery, which is for less valuable and less urgent letters. Both Special Delivery and Recorded Delivery require that the recipient signs to say that the letter has been received.

Personal letters | 2

Personal letters are not such common forms of communication today as they used to be because various other methods have superseded them in many instances. Telephone, texting, e-mail and various other internet-based communication possibilities, such as instant messaging, are often easier, usually quicker and sometimes seem more direct. Nevertheless, there is something very appealing, more intimate and personal about receiving a letter handwritten by someone you know well. Especially if you have written to someone to convey some deeply held opinions or feelings, it is much better that they have the letter to read and reread, and then they can reply, if necessary, having carefully considered what you said. Letters are also more satisfactory for getting in touch with someone you have not seen or spoken to for a while. Even if they have moved, the letter is quite likely to be forwarded.

A personal letter can also be something to treasure, and to reread in years to come. People often keep love letters, although they can sometimes provide sad or uncomfortable memories. It is very important to consider carefully what you are going to say in a personal letter, because of its permanent nature. If you write something you don't really believe, you may regret it, and the recipient will have the evidence! On the other hand, a letter is the best form of communication if you want to express something sincerely. Any genuine sentiment expressed in a letter is likely to be appreciated much more by the recipient than if it was delivered in some other way.

Some thoughts on personal e-mails

E-mail and other forms of electronic text communication are ideal for informal communication, especially when you want an immediate response. They can also be more like a conversation, and, of course, they have revolutionised international communication, making it flexible and immediate.

Be aware, though, that e-mails are notorious for causing misunderstandings, largely because you cannot always tell the tone when the language is often very concise; hence the rise of the emoticon, much despised in some quarters. An emoticon is an arrangement of punctuation symbols to create 'faces' displaying various emotions such as anger or surprise (see page 248). Do be aware that your quick 'No – can't come' could easily be read as an angry snub, even if that is not what you intended.

Keeping in touch

The following are a few examples of general personal letters. It is important to pitch the level of personal detail correctly. It is inappropriate to reveal intimate information to people you know only superficially, but being too reserved with close friends will appear cold and unfriendly. Be chatty and informative, and ask them about themselves to invite a reply and to avoid seeming self-centred. Ideally, be spontaneous, rather than planning the letter carefully. Your aim should be to appear natural, and if you try too hard to get it right the style may seem artificial, somewhat undermining the character of a supposedly personal letter. Personal letters can, of course, be a medium for expressing concerns on a variety of matters.

38 Rolleson Road
Barford
London
SE45 6GN
4 January 20—

Dear Cicely

It seems rather a long time now since we were walking in Wales, and I was just thinking about you, wondering how you are. City life has its good points, but I really miss the great outdoors and the fresh air. Did any of your photos come out well? I hope there weren't any embarrassing ones of me!

Work is still a little stressful, and I'm still looking around for something better. Did you ever get any positive news about the book? I'd certainly like to be involved in something more creative. Sitting at a desk all day doing the same old thing over and over again is hardly inspiring, and I'm sure it makes me more tired.

I saw Belinda the other day and she asked after you. Of course, I had to say I didn't know anything, and I felt rather guilty – hence this letter! She was looking well and apparently has a new man. She didn't tell me much, probably because she's not too sure where it's going. No doubt she'll let me know if there are any developments.

My sister is still acting, although she seems a bit fed up with it. I think she'd like to be on the other side of the fence, directing plays. I tell her to be patient, because she hasn't really been in the theatre that long, but she's always been restless by nature.

I'd really like to hear your news. Perhaps we could arrange to meet up for lunch soon – you could come here or, if it seems too far, perhaps at a pub somewhere. It would be nice if you could make it over here, because I'd love to show you my garden, and you could meet Tom (my cat, in case you thought my love life had improved!). If it is too far just for lunch, why not come for the weekend?

Love Jane

67 Ambleford Court
Rochester
Kent
FN5 8TY
8 June 20–

Dear John

I thought I should write to you because your mother has expressed her concern to me about your plans to move to Newcastle for the new job. She was worried about telling me this, in case you thought she was going behind your back and revealing 'secrets', but I told her I already knew about the possibility. I think she's a bit frightened about being left somewhat isolated in Kent, although I assured her that her many friends, including us, would always be there to support her. I also said that it's not really that much of a problem for you to get back reasonably quickly with the motorways and trains and planes.

Anyway, I'm sure you were aware of how she was likely to be feeling, but if she's hiding it well, I thought maybe I should let you know that she needs a bit of reassurance. Not easy I know! You do really need to put your career first, because you'll always regret it if you don't make the move, and if you consider your mother's needs before your own, you'll only end up resenting her for it.

One possibility I thought of is for you to move her up there with you, not necessarily to live with you, but to be nearby. She probably wouldn't agree with this, because I know she likes it where she is, but it's probably something to consider. The only problem with that is that she really would be dependent on you, because she would have left all her friends behind.

If you need any support from me, whether by me talking to her or just listening to you over a pint in the King's Head, let me know.

All the best

Arthur

Greenacres
Barn Close
Garshiel
Ayrshire
AY5 2BF
14 May 20–

Dear Astrid

I think I rather put my foot in it last night when we were round for dinner. Please accept my apologies. It was very thoughtless of me, and I have really no excuse, except to say that I'd probably had a little too much to drink. I really don't think what I said is true, and I am thoroughly ashamed of myself. I very much hope we can put it behind us and stay friends. I hope Amanda will understand as well. If you want me to explain to her, please let me know.

Sincerely

George

Expressing appreciation

5 Smith Avenue
Bartown
Powys
WL5 3QL
4 January 20–

Dear Rajiv

You can't possibly know how much our conversation last week has meant to me. To find someone else who thinks the same way as I do was really encouraging, and at last I don't feel isolated in my wild imaginings, which are obviously not so wild after all! I feel really uplifted, and it's good to start a new year in such a frame of mind. I look forward to our next meeting. Is the 11th still okay for you?

Best wishes

Tadeusz

The Mansion
Park Avenue
Leeds
West Yorkshire
L19 3RR
14 December 20–

Hello everybody

It's been another very busy year for us, so we hope that you're not offended if we haven't been in touch. Hopefully, we'll put that right in the New Year.

Robert began a new job in March, and it's very satisfying. It's great for him to feel that he's actually making a difference. Fortunately, he's under less pressure to work long hours, which means he spends more time with the family. June is still busy at the shop, and she still enjoys it immensely. Customers come from far and wide, and she often has people coming over 30 miles because they've heard from friends what a wonderful range of gifts she has. It's nice to be appreciated!

The children are still working hard at school, and we're generally very pleased with them and the school. Alice is coming up to her GCSEs and is getting a little bit worked up about it. Fortunately, she has a good set of friends who are all in the same boat, of course, and they're very sensible about dividing time between work and play. John is as usual very sport-orientated, and has been particularly successful both in football and in cricket this year, with both teams trouncing the opposition in spectacular style. But he still devotes plenty of time to academic work.

We had a good holiday in Tunisia in the summer – a mix of lazing on the beach, seeing the sights and desert trekking. In February, we're off skiing as usual, but this year a bit farther afield in the Canadian Rockies.

Hope you have a good Christmas and a Happy New Year.

Robert, June, Alice and John

This can be simple, as in the example below, or used as an opportunity to renew an acquaintance by including some news, as in the general communication on page 38.

16 Station Road
Hartley
Ripon
North Yorkshire
RR5 3ER
6 May 20–

Dear Mr and Mrs Armstrong

Please note our new address from 29 May:

16 Willmore Gardens
Hartley
Ripon
North Yorkshire
RR6 7TG
Telephone 01234 567890

Yours sincerely

Peter and Janet Nayland

Good luck and congratulations

These sample letters are easy to adapt to any message of good luck or congratulation. Try to make sure you make a personal mention of something important or relevant so the recipient knows you are thinking specifically of them.

Good luck with a driving test

> 29 Eden Drive
> Bossthwaite
> Yorkshire
> SK3 6BD
> 20 July 20–

Dear Jim

I just wanted to wish you the best of luck with the driving test – not that you need it, of course! Just stay calm and give the examiner a nice smile.

I look forward to you giving me a lift in to the match next Saturday.

All the best

David

Good luck with an examination

> 7 Abbots Close
> Hatton
> London
> NW1 2SV
> 19 June 20–

Dear Jemima

We understand your exams begin next Tuesday and we want to wish you the very best of luck. Try not to be nervous and get a good night's sleep before each one! We know you've prepared well and deserve to get good results. Just think, it won't be long before they're over and then you can relax.

Love Boris and Judy

Congratulations on passing the driving test

7 Northolt Street
Authors Green
Heathcote
Derbyshire
DE15 2SV
20 December 20–

Dearest Lysette

We were so pleased to hear that you've passed your driving test, and at the first attempt. Well done, indeed! I expect your parents are very pleased and your Mum is looking forward to you taking her out to the sales in January!

Love and best wishes

Mary and Roger

Congratulations on passing examinations

51 Church Street
Patchett St Giles
Wiltshire
CH3 9XD
8 August 20–

Dear Sanjay

I just heard the fantastic news from your Mum. You must be very pleased with the results. Really, to get eight A grades is quite an achievement. Congratulations!

What are your plans for A level?

All the best

Marius

Relationships

Love letters are the most highly personal of all forms of correspondence and it would be a mistake to try to lay down any rules for this sort of writing. There is only one worthwhile rule and that is simply: be yourself. Write naturally and without any affectation. Do not try for any highly literary style or your letters will sound unnatural. The best thing is to write to your loved one in the way that you talk.

A word of warning, however: beware of making a definite promise in writing that you may not want to keep. Love is a matter of emotions, but do not allow yourself to be carried away by your feelings and lose your common sense.

The normal rules for beginning and ending letters do not apply to love letters. All couples have their own favourite ways, and in fact originality is half the charm of a love letter. 'My dearest Joe', 'My darling Becky' or any greeting using a pet name are all good openings in the appropriate circumstances. The word 'love' cannot very well be left out of the ending, although the exact wording of this is entirely a matter of taste and using simply 'Love' followed by your name is not very special.

Do not overdo the endearments or they will begin to lose their value. Send kisses by all means, but decorating half a page with *xxxx* can look rather cheap and silly. If you have done it on one letter, you may feel that you have to do it on every one, and then if you stop doing it, your lover may think there is something wrong! Certainly, do not put any signs or symbols of endearment on the envelope; making somebody embarrassed in front of the postman or another member of the family is hardly likely to sustain your relationship.

Proposals of marriage

Proposals of marriage are almost invariably made verbally and it is far better this way than by writing, for reasons that should be obvious. Shyness is a poor excuse and even a stammered proposal is more likely to be favourably received than a beautifully written letter. Anyone who writes instead of speaks because he fears a refusal is likely to get the refusal he fears.

So a proposal should only be made by letter when there are special circumstances that make a verbal proposal impossible. The most common reason is when the two parties are separated by hundreds or thousands of miles. If it is impossible to overcome this – as it may be, for example, when the separation is due to service in the forces, or overseas employment – then a letter is perhaps justified.

Courtship by correspondence requires just as much thought as the more normal form of relationship involving actual dating and going out together. Most likely, the man and woman will have already been out together a few times and are getting to know each other more through their letters. It could be that they eventually reveal enough to each other to indicate that theirs will not be a long-term relationship. But perhaps they will realise more and more through their correspondence that they are meant for each other.

The form of the letter containing the proposal will naturally depend to a great extent on the previous correspondence. The important thing is that there should not be any noticeable change of style and therefore the following example should be modified with this in mind. The proposal here is from the man, but there is no reason why the letter should not be modified to be from the woman. With more equality between the sexes, it's by no means guaranteed that the woman will travel to be with the man. It is quite likely that hers is the more high-powered job.

3 Chiswick Terrace
Bristol
BS8 5TK
18 March 20–

Darling Jen

Monday again – and another dreary Monday, because I've got to wait five long days before I see you again. I would be feeling utterly miserable if I hadn't got so many wonderful hopes and memories to keep me company. And after all, it was only yesterday when we were together, so I really shouldn't grumble.

Jenny dearest, I tried to tell you last night how much I love you and I don't think I said half of what I really meant. I thought I might make up for that in this letter – and now I'm even more stuck for words. I'll have another go next weekend!

As you will guess, I'm writing this in my lunch-hour and old Tom Smith is peering over his half-moon specs, hoping to see what I'm up to, but trying hard not to let me know it. I wonder if he ever wrote letters like this to Mrs S. It's hard to believe!

It's just coming up to two o'clock now, so I must stop and get back to the grindstone. Goodbye, my darling. I'll write again before Saturday. I think of you all the time.

Your own loving

Daniel

340 Longland Road
Gloucester
G10 5BZ
22 March 20–

My dearest Daniel

Mum keeps giving me funny looks when your letters arrive, and even the postman seems to notice that that I'm getting lots of mail from the same person. But that's probably just my imagination! Dad goes on reading the paper or his book and pretends not to notice.

I hate to think of you sitting in that office with only Tom to keep you company. But it's the same for me, you know. My days at work are just as boring as yours, although Bob Taylor does make the odd funny remark sometimes. He also mentioned what a nice bracelet I was wearing this morning. 'Is it a new one?' he asked casually, but I think he was dying to know who had given it to me. He's not the only one who's said things in the past few weeks – that's the trouble with open-plan offices: you can never keep anything secret.

Darling, I'm just as fed up waiting for weekends as you are, but I feel a lot better when I get your letters. I've got quite a collection of them now and they've all been read lots of times.

You know I'm not very good at expressing my feelings either, especially in letters – but you do know that I love you, don't you, Dan? Because I do – more than I can say.

Your own

Jenny

20 Acacia Avenue
Keyworth
Nottingham
NG12 7TY
18 December 20–

Dearest Tom

I know it's only tomorrow when we will see each other again, and when you will get this letter, but I really had to put something down in words. I feel so hopeless about expressing the way I feel when we're together. I really don't want to lose you because you don't know how I feel!

You have brought more joy than I can ever express in words. The sound of your voice makes my heart sing. I love every little thing about you – your sexy smile, the magic in your eyes, even your smell. I love your gentle touch and the warmth I feel at your side. I love dreaming about you and daydreaming about you. Every moment I share with you seems a once-in-a-lifetime moment. I want to be near you all the time. You make me feel so safe in your arms. You are the most wonderful thing that ever happened to me and when I look into your eyes I'm lost in a world of magic and love.

Can I possibly wait until the next time we're together? It'll be tomorrow, when you get this letter, a whole 24 hours away. It doesn't seem possible to get through them, but I suppose I will. I love you just because I do. I really never thought I'd ever feel this way. I didn't believe that love for me was possible. So I need to thank you for everything and being you. You have taught me how to love.

Until tomorrow then (I mean this evening!).

Your loving, loving Andrea

Flat 5
Cadogan Court
High Street
Walworth
Hertfordshire
HH15 6RT
19 December 20–

My darling Andrea

I'm not sure I'll post this, because there doesn't seem any point as we'll see each other in a few hours, so I'll probably just give it to you. I just wanted to say how wonderful it was to receive your letter. I'm truly overwhelmed by what you say, but you've no need to worry, I know how you feel and you're really not going to lose me. I'm totally committed to our relationship because I feel just the same about you. It feels so awful to be parted from you even for a second, let alone two whole days. Soon we'll be together again, and that's how it should be, for ever.

I love you, I love you, I love you.

Tom

PO Box No 525
Mumbai
India
4 June 20–

My dearest Emma

I don't know how many times I have complained in my letters about our continued separation and I think that you have guessed by now that there is a pretty deep reason behind this complaint. This separation is even worse at the moment than it has ever been because, darling, I really don't think I can put off any longer asking you a question that I had been hoping to ask in different circumstances. I expect you know what is coming, so here goes. Will you marry me?

You know that I love you and since we parted two months ago my feelings have grown even stronger. I couldn't ask you then, because we hadn't known each other long and in any case I expected to be home again soon. I meant to wait until I got back – but I just can't.

I know that I can't offer you much – not even myself just now – and I've no idea how much longer I'll be stuck out here. But there must be an end to it soon, and the waiting will be less difficult if I can think that the end will also be a beginning – of a new life with you as my wife.

I'd probably have said it differently if we had been together, but it isn't easy to express feelings of this sort in a letter. I only hope you can read between the lines and guess just how much I really love and want you.

Yours for ever, if you want me, darling,

Richard

49 Oakfields Road
Bath
Somerset
BA12 8NQ
19 June 20–

My dearest Richard

Yes, yes, YES!

Do I sound too eager and worried that you might change your mind? I hope not. I'm sure this isn't a sudden decision on your part, and the truth is I was expecting it. You gave me a pretty broad hint in your last letter – and when I replied I tried to give you the green light. In fact, I made up my mind weeks ago. Perhaps I should even have asked you first!

Richard, I know we can't fix a date and I'm as fed up about this separation as you are. It's no good asking you to be patient, because I'm really impatient myself. We must just hope and dream.

Mum and Dad are writing to you separately – but I can tell you now that they are very pleased. I can't tell you how I feel – at the moment I'm just over the moon with excitement and can't even eat. I think of you all the time and dream about our future together. To say I'm on cloud nine just doesn't come near it! Darling Richard, I love you so very much.

I'll write again when I've calmed down a bit. Until then, dearest,

Yours for ever

Emma

49 Oakfields Road
Bath
Somerset
BA12 8NQ
19 June 20–

My dear Richard

You have paid me the greatest compliment any woman can receive and the least I can do is to give you a direct answer. And, Richard, I am afraid the answer is no.

Reading your letter made me feel very guilty. It never occurred to me that you were leading up to this in your previous letters and if I seemed to give you encouragement I assure you it was not intended. If we had been seeing each other instead of just writing I'm sure this would never have happened.

I should at least give you a reason for refusing. It would be easy for me to say that we hadn't known each other long enough or that I'm not really sure about my feelings towards you. But that would be unfair. It might make you go on wasting your hopes on me, and they really would be wasted.

Richard, please don't take it too much to heart when I say I don't want to marry you. I like you tremendously – more than any other man I know. But I'm not in love with you, and – please don't be hurt – I never shall be.

Richard, I like and admire you and you mustn't feel bad. I've risked hurting your feelings because I don't want you to waste your time hoping that I'll change when I know I won't. And I know you'll move on in your life and find someone much better for you than me.

I hope you will always think of me as

Your very sincere friend

Emma

Only send this sort of letter if you really mean it. It's not fair to keep someone hanging on for an answer that they are never going to get.

49 Oakfields Road
Bath
Somerset
BA12 8NQ
19 June 20—

My dear Richard

I have just received your letter asking me to marry you, and feel I should now write back yes or no. But the trouble is, Richard, I can't. I like you very much, you know that, but I honestly don't know whether I love you. I didn't know you long enough while you were still in England and I won't really know how I feel until I see you again in person.

The other side of the coin is that you might find that I'm not quite as you imagine I am. You probably haven't gained a clear idea from our brief time together and my letters. I'd hate you to come back and find that you didn't love your fiancée after all.

If I seemed to encourage you to make a proposal, I'm sorry. I didn't mean to.

I know that this 'she didn't say yes, didn't say no' line is unsatisfactory and I know that I may regret it. But I can't see any alternative.

May I make a suggestion? Let's go on writing to each other as before and see how it works out. But no ties yet. If either of us meets someone else, the other has no claim. There's one more thing, Richard. I haven't met anyone else yet. But if I do I'll tell you at once. I expect you to do the same, for both our sakes.

Yours ever

Emma

Writing a letter after a row can be far better than a telephone call. The person receiving the call may be taken by surprise and simply slam down the receiver, which will only make matters worse!

137 Meadfoot Road
Bradley
Devon
BD22 1PT
9 July 20—

Darling

Will you forgive – and forget?

I was a fool last night and I know it. I can't imagine why I said what I did and I am kicking myself for being so stupid.

This is the first time we have quarrelled and I am determined that it will be the last. I've never felt so miserable in my life.

When can I come and see you again?

Your loving

Ed

Reply to the above letter of apology

68 Chesserton Road
Bradley
Devon
BD15 9XU
10 July 20—

My dearest Ed

It is forgotten as far as I am concerned. I don't need to forgive you, because you were not the only one to blame. It takes two to make a quarrel and I played my part, too.

As you say, it was our first quarrel and I agree we should try to make it the last. I was feeling very miserable until your letter came.

Please come round as soon as you can.

Your loving

Pam

78 Marchmont Drive
Gloucester Road
London
SW3 4PB
8 September 20–

My dearest Beth

We've always agreed to be honest with each other and I'm not going to pretend to be full of abject apologies because I don't feel it. You were angry with me and, as I said at the time, I thought you were unfair. I still think so, but I realise that I did not help matters by the way I reacted.

I don't mind admitting that I've felt pretty fed up since our row. I want to make it up, but I know you wouldn't think much of me if I tried to get round you by taking all the blame. I reckon it's about fifty-fifty and I hope you'll agree to forget the whole thing.

Darling, I love you as much as I ever did. When can we see each other and kiss and make up?

Your loving

Jonathan

49 Doncaster Street
London
N20 9KU
10 September 20–

My dearest Jonathan

You've made me feel absolutely awful. I've been trying to write to you ever since Saturday and it was only stupid false pride that prevented me. It would have served me right if I'd lost you.

I don't agree that the blame was fifty-fifty, or anything like that. It was all my fault, but if it's any consolation to you I've felt utterly miserable ever since.

I think you're wonderful and I don't deserve you. Please come over as soon as you can for that make-up kiss.

Your loving

Beth

36 Ditton Hill Lane
Charlton
Stafford
S15 9BQ
15 January 20–

Dear Harry

This is a very sad letter to have to write and I assure you that I have given it many bitter hours, if not days or weeks, of consideration.

I'm sorry to say that I've come to the conclusion that we are not right for each other and to marry in these circumstances would be wrong.

I think that the only sensible plan is for us to part and so I am writing to break off our engagement.

You have always been wonderful to me and I admire you very much. But to be honest, I have come to feel that it is not love that has brought us together.

I know this will hurt you and it is hurting me to write it, but we must be sensible and face up to things as they really are. To continue would only make things more painful.

Yours sincerely

Danuta

Thank-you letters

Thank-you letters are for a specific purpose, and so do not need to be very long. You need to show that you appreciate the gift or what has been done for you, and that you value the connection with the person concerned, so make sure you keep the letter personal.

Thanks for a birthday present

763 Archerhill Street
Glasgow
G3 4EB
20 February 20–

Dear David

It was really nice of you to remember my birthday and even nicer that you sent me the bottle of whisky. Believe it or not we didn't have a single drop in the house, so your present arrived just at the right moment. And single malt as well – not like our usual rubbish!

Tell your mum that it's so long since she last came to see us we're beginning to wonder if she's forgotten us. Why not bring her over next Sunday?

All the best

Uncle Bob

Child's thank-you letter for a birthday present

803 Coalville Road
Edgbaston
Birmingham
B3 9DN
19 January 20–

Dear Mrs Watson

Thank you very much for the book token you sent me for my birthday. I'm always running out of books to read, and it'll be nice to be able to go to the bookshop with some extra money to spend.

I had lots of nice presents. Mum and Dad bought me the iPod I'd asked for, so I was really excited by that. I had to promise that I wouldn't use it while doing my homework though!

Best wishes

Elizabeth

Child's thank-you letter for a Christmas present

3 Sycamore Road
Brinklow
Northampton
NN3 9DN
19 January 20—

Dear Uncle Jim and Auntie Betty

Thank you very much for the Muse CDs. How did you know they are my favourite band? I had a lot of other nice Christmas presents, including several books, some paints and a chemistry set, but really this was my best present apart from the ones Mum and Dad bought me. Did you hear about the guitar they got me? My friends at school will all be jealous. I play the CDs all the time, and Mum and Dad keep telling me to turn the volume down!

I hope Tom had a nice lot of presents and that he enjoyed Christmas as much as I did.

Love

Michael

Thanks for a wedding present

Flat 15
38 Victoria Mansions
London
W21 5XR
18 June 20—

Dear Julia

It was very kind of you to send us such a lovely wedding present. I really don't know how to thank you. Derek is as pleased with the food processor as I am.

We are looking forward to seeing you on the great day and hope Richard will be able to come as well. We're all very busy with the preparations, but I'm really happy.

Thank you very much.

Love Sally

14 Armour Street
Cardiff
CF4 3DT
10 June 20–

Dear Mrs Mikolajski

Just wanted to thank you for inviting John to Lucinda's birthday party. He enjoyed it very much and told me all about the games they played. I hope there wasn't too much clearing up to do afterwards! We were particularly touched that you invited him because, having just moved to the area, he is finding it a little difficult to adjust and to make new friends. Perhaps Lucinda would like to come round to tea some time. Please let me know if she would like to, and we can fix a date.

Yours sincerely

Tom Goldfeld

Thanks for being taken out

29 Farmer Street
Belfast
BT4 5QR
14 June 20–

Dear Tony

Thanks very much for taking Rod to the seaside on Thursday. He really enjoys being with Sid and Mary and I think he'd say they are his best friends. I'm sorry we can't reciprocate more often. We're so busy with the shop these days, and unfortunately it takes up most of our weekends as well.

We're very pleased with the way the school dealt with that bullying incident recently, as no doubt you are. Although our children were not directly involved, it's comforting to hear that it was stamped on quite firmly.

Best wishes

Martha Jones

Ballington Grange
Denton
Hartlepool
County Durham
TS45 5TY
12 September 20–

Dear Patricia

Just to say that Ben told us he had a lovely time when he came to stay in August. Thank you very much for inviting him. It was great for him to get a bit of sunshine away from the rather dull environment that we live in! Don't think I'm complaining too much, though – Hartlepool has its good points. There is plenty to do around here, and I wonder if James would like to come at half-term.

It's nice for the two of them to be able to keep in touch, even though we're so far away from each other. It would be good to see you and Bill as well, and we'd be glad to put you up if you could spare the time.

Let me know when you can.

All the best

Jill

Family matters 3

This chapter deals with subjects connected particularly with children, education and family issues. Many communications around family matters are quite intimate, and so can have a very informal nature. Others are more formal and as such tend to follow an accepted form that might seem a little old-fashioned, but it is generally what people expect, so don't worry about appearing out of touch with the modern way of doing things.

Births, special birthdays and anniversaries

Sometimes you will simply send a greetings card, but for a very special occasion or someone particularly close to you, it is far nicer to send a handwritten letter. People will often keep such letters and cards and enjoy rereading them many times.

Announcing a birth

56 Glendower Court
Gloucester
GL9 5EU
3 June 20–

Dear Miss Fulford

I just wanted to let you know about the birth of our son – as yet unnamed! – on 2 June 20– at the Simpson Maternity Hospital in Gloucester. He weighed 8 pounds 5 ounces. Both Susan and the baby are doing very well.

Yours sincerely

Geoffrey Hillman

Reply to a birth announcement

64 Cedarwood Terrace
Westbourne Grove
London
W2 5PR
8 June 20–

Dear Mr Hillman

I was delighted to learn from your letter that you and Susan have a son. You must both feel very proud.

Please give my love to Susan and tell her I am so glad she is feeling well. I should love to come and see her when I may.

It was extremely kind of you to let me know, especially as you must be finding life rather busy at the moment.

Yours sincerely

Barbara Fulford

Tessington Manor House
Telford
Shropshire
GU3 2RS
5 March 20–

My dear Mrs Patel

Please accept my congratulations to you on becoming a grandmother. I was so pleased to hear that Parvati had started off with a son and I am told that he is a very healthy and happy boy! How proud you must be! I am dying to see Parvati and the boy. Have they decided on a name yet? I am so glad to know that Parvati has Angela Billing for a nanny. I believe she is excellent.

I hope you are quite well, and that the rest of the family are in the best of health.

Yours sincerely

Mrs Anita Chowdry

To a friend on his birthday

73 Marchmont Drive
Cambuslang
Glasgow
G15 9XP
18 February 20–

Dear Giles

I'm writing to wish you a very happy birthday tomorrow. I'm sorry I won't be there to celebrate with you, but I hope the enclosed will help the evening go with a swing.

Mary sends her good wishes as well. She says she'd have made you a cake except that you don't like them, apparently. Anyway, it's the thought that counts!

All the best

Roger

The Limes
Kingswood Avenue
Chesterton
Surrey
CH9 3PT
31 March 20–

Dear Vivienne

I want to send you my congratulations on your Coming of Age next Friday. I hope it will be a very happy and memorable day for you.

I enclose a small gift, which I hope you will like.

Love and best wishes

Aunt Dorothy

Congratulations on a silver wedding

14 Grant Street
Angmering
Sussex
AG4 3DT
10 June 20–

Dear Joe

I'm sure you haven't forgotten that it was 25 years ago tomorrow that I was best man at your wedding. At the reception I proposed the health of Mary and yourself and expressed the hope that you would have many happy years together. Now you will be celebrating the occasion together, and you have every reason to feel pleased with yourselves. Every marriage has its ups and downs, but I'm sure I can truthfully say that there haven't been many downs in yours.

Sally joins me in wishing you many more years of happiness together. We enclose a little gift to mark the occasion, and I hope that we'll be able to send you another one in gold in 25 years' time.

All good wishes

Tom

29 Neil Street
London
W4 5QR
14 June 20–

Dear Tom

Thanks for thinking of us on our silver wedding day. Your stunning gift is in a place of honour on our dresser, just next to the present you gave us 25 years ago, which has lasted as well as we have. You're right – not many upsets in our marriage!

It was almost exactly three years after that day that I had the pleasure of being your best man, and I look forward to returning your congratulations when you join us in this 'silvered respectability'.

Mary joins me in thanking you both and wishing you continuing happiness in the future.

Yours truly

Joe

Congratulations on a golden wedding

The Haven
Seaburn
Dorset
SB5 7JN
3 November 20–

Dear Mr and Mrs Fox

My wife and I wish to offer you our sincere congratulations on your Golden Wedding anniversary, which I understand is tomorrow.

No doubt you will be casting your minds back to various incidents in your married life and we are sure the thoughts will give you a great deal of pleasure. You have indeed had a fortunate time together, but that is only what you both deserve.

May life continue to be happy for you and may you both enjoy each other's company for many, many years to come.

Yours sincerely

Bill and Sylvia Thomas

Engagements and weddings

You may inform your broader circle of friends by putting an announcement in the newspaper, but it is preferable to let family and close friends know first, either by speaking with them or by sending a personal letter.

Announcing an engagement

52 Cherry Gardens
Portsmouth
Hampshire
PO2 3BL
17 April 20–

Dear Auntie

I am writing to tell you some wonderful news. David and I have decided to get married!

We are not planning a long engagement, so the wedding will be in the next few months. We shall send you an invitation as soon as we have the date and the place sorted out.

I do hope you will be able to come.

Love

Alison

Congratulating a woman on her engagement

53 Locksley Mansions
London
SW21 9LY
31 March 20–

Dear Anne

I have been hearing all sorts of rumours linking your name with a certain army officer, and today I have been told outright that you and he are engaged. Let me be one of the first to offer you my congratulations. Needless to say, he is a very lucky man and he should be congratulated, too.

You will make a wonderful wife when the time comes and I look forward to visiting you in your new home.

I hope you will both be very happy.

Yours sincerely

Brenda

Congratulating a man on his engagement

45 High Stack
Barmore
Inverness
IV2 4RT
E-mail: john.silver@bestway.co.uk
30 June 20–

Dear Alex

Just heard that you and Sarah have got engaged. Congratulations! She's a lovely girl. I wish I could find one like her! Have you set a date for the wedding yet?

My parents send their best wishes to you. They found out before I did! 'Heard it through the grapevine', as the song goes.

Anyway, it would be great to hear your plans. Drop me a line or send an e-mail when you can. Perhaps we could meet up when I'm in Glasgow some time.

All the best

John

This letter could, of course, be adapted to be about a son's engagement.

364 Sloan Drive
Ipswich
Suffolk
IP1 9UT
15 May 20–

Dear Mr and Mrs Durrant

I was delighted to read in today's Daily Telegraph of the engagement of your daughter Sophie to Harry Egremont.

I am writing to congratulate both you and Sophie and I trust she will be very happy. It is certainly something to make you feel proud. Arthur and I met Harry once briefly, and he struck us as being a very nice young man.

Arthur joins with me in sending our kind regards both to you and to your husband.

Yours very sincerely

Mary Cohen

Allinson Grange
Polpeard
Cornwall
PZ4 5TO
12 September 20–

My dear Patricia

William has written and told me of his great happiness in his
engagement to you, but I feel that I'm not able to share his feelings
properly until I have met you and welcomed you into the family as
my 'new daughter'.

He tells me that he can get away from work for a few days on the
28th, so I am writing to ask you whether you could come to stay with
us then, so that we can all get to know you. We'd also like to meet
your parents very soon.

William will only be able to stay for a few days, but if you would
like to stay longer, we'd be delighted to have you with us for the rest
of the week. Megan and Janet are also very keen to meet you, so
please come if you can.

I look forward to hearing from you.

Yours sincerely

Mary Woodrow

14 Castle Street
Hendon
London
NW10 5BP
15 September 20–

Dear Mrs Woodrow

It is very kind of you to write and ask me to visit you. I'll be pleased
to come on the 28th, and I'm really looking forward to meeting you.

Unfortunately, I'm also unable to take too much time off work at the
moment, so I'll only be able to stay for two days, but I am sure that
will give us the opportunity to begin to get to know each other.

Tell Megan and Janet that I'm also keen to meet them, because I've
heard so much about them.

Yours sincerely

Patricia

The following is to parents of a man who clearly has a good relationship with them. Some rewording may be necessary if that is not the case!

Flat 23
Savoy Court
Whitehaven
Cumbria
CA30 4YZ
29 July 20–

Dear Mr and Mrs Armstrong

As you know, James and I have decided to marry, and I'm writing to you to tell you how much I'm looking forward to meeting you. I'm sorry that it hasn't been possible so far, but the distances involved and my work commitments have made it all rather difficult.

James and I have been together now for more than a year, and we really feel we were made for each other. He has told me so much about you and I'm very excited at the prospect of being a member of your family.

Yours sincerely

Siobhan O'Farrell

Announcement of a wedding

Wedding invitations tend to be formal and sent out on printed cards. The form of words is fairly standard, and printing firms generally offer a choice of styles. The following is a letter written to announce a wedding that the recipients are not being invited to because it is to be simple ceremony with no formal reception, possibly because the family cannot afford one or for some other reason.

Announcement of a wedding

> 34 Tramore Gardens
> Pilsden
> Derbyshire
> DE34 5TY
> 12 April 20–

Dear Mark and Belinda

Alison and I wanted to let you know that Graham and Debbie have decided to get married. It will be a quiet wedding, with only the family and a few of Graham and Debbie's closest friends, which is what they have requested.

We hope to be able to celebrate their marriage with a more informal party some time in the near future.

Yours sincerely

Alfred Ransome

Reply to a formal wedding invitation

These are always in the third person.

> The Red Roofs
> Mexford
> Lancashire
> MX2 9BD
> 20 February 20–

Miss Lucy Thompson thanks Dr and Mrs Mervyn Giles for their kind invitation to be present at the wedding of their daughter Susan to Mr Graham Jones, which she has much pleasure in accepting.

OR

Miss Lucy Thompson has much pleasure in accepting the kind invitation of Dr and Mrs Mervyn Giles to be present at the wedding of their daughter Susan to Mr Graham Jones.

5 Cedar Court
Cedar Avenue
Carlisle
Cumbria
CA2 4YZ
29 July 20–

Dear Milan

Your wedding announcement letter reached me this morning and I send you my hearty congratulations.

As I have not yet met Angela, I will take for granted all that you have said about her, but I hope to meet her soon! Any time you are in the area, please drop by, or perhaps we could arrange to meet somewhere in London when I'm down.

Where are you planning to live? Surely not in your pokey flat!

Give my best wishes to Angela.

All the best

Ted

Congratulating a woman on her marriage

31 Selwyn Gardens
Blandford Forum
Dorset
BL15 2QP
16 April 20–

Dear Felicity

It seems that all the nice girls are getting married and now I hear that you too have taken the plunge. My mother and I wish you both a great deal of happiness and we send our congratulations.

We should love to meet Jim and so we hope you will bring him to see us one day very soon.

There is a small present enclosed, which Mother and I are sending with our best wishes to you both.

Yours sincerely

Arthur

All about school

This set of sample letters can easily be adapted to suit different communications with the school or the teachers. However, there are plenty of opportunities to talk with your child's teacher if there is an issue you wish to discuss, especially at primary school, and this can sometimes be the best option.

Requesting a school prospectus

34 King Edward Mews
Windsor
Berkshire
SL4 9IK
31 May 20–

The Secretary
Peveril Hill School
Stanton
Hants
BS9 7TW

Dear Madam

We shall shortly be moving to Stanton and are therefore looking for a suitable school for our daughters, aged 12 and 14. Peveril Hill School has been highly praised by our friends, Mr and Mrs John Adamson, whose daughter Patricia is a pupil at present.

I should be pleased if you would send me a prospectus of the school, together with any information you have about arranging a visit to the school.

Yours faithfully

Gerald Gray

24 Northwood Avenue
Bristol
BS4 8TF
29 September 20–

Dr W. R. Weston
Headmaster
Shipley Court Preparatory School
Fawley Lane
Long Melford
Suffolk
IP12 4ST

Dear Dr Weston

Our son Mark was born on 28 June of this year and I am writing to register his name for entrance as a boarding pupil at Shipley Court for the year starting September 20–.

As you know, I attended Shipley Court myself, as did my father, and I consider that the educational and sporting facilities it offers are quite exceptional.

We should prefer Mark to join Askins, my old house.

My best wishes to Mrs Weston.

Yours sincerely

Peter M. Hayward

80 Fulwell Road
Preston
Lancashire
PR6 4XB
3 March 20–

Mrs R. M. Turner
Head Teacher
St Mary's Junior School
Hill Green
Preston
Lancashire
PR6 2BL

Dear Mrs Turner

My daughter Susan is returning to school today, after nearly a week's absence. She has been suffering from a chest infection and so it seemed advisable to keep her at home.

She is much better now and I will encourage her to do what she can to make up for lost time. Please ask her teachers to advise her about any extra work she may need to do to catch up.

Yours sincerely

Jean Wormald

66 Goldsmith Road
Highfields
Westerham
Kent
WH2 9VL
19 February 20–

Mrs J. Worsley
Head Teacher
Westerham Middle School
Westerham
Kent
WH2 8TV

Dear Mrs Worsley

I am sorry that my daughter Kylie was unable to do her homework
last night.

Unfortunately, she came home at teatime with a bad headache and
she had to go to bed, so she was unable to do the work set.

Yours sincerely

Mary Simmonds

Request for a child to be excused from religious instruction

15 Woodside Close
Berryford
West Sussex
BN3 3HH
21 April 20–

Ms S. Butcher
Head Teacher
Berryford School
Berryford
West Sussex
BN3 4PD

Dear Ms Butcher

Our son Surinder is to be a pupil at your school from September of
this year and I am taking this opportunity to request that he be
excused from religious instruction.

Although he was born in this country, he has been raised in the Sikh faith and receives instruction according to our own religion.

Yours sincerely

Dalip Singh

Request for a child to be excused from sex education

The Barn
Owl Close
Pilkington
Leicestershire
LE13 3TT
21 August 20–

T. T. Ripley Esq
Headmaster
Alderman Thwaite School
Pilkington
Leicestershire
LE13 4RE

Dear Mr Ripley

Our daughter Rebecca will move into Mr Dunnett's class at your school soon and I am writing to say that I wish her to be excused from the proposed sex education classes this autumn.

My wife and I feel that this is an issue that we can quite adequately deal with ourselves when the time is right.

Yours sincerely

F. R. Saunders

This can be amended for any sport or outdoor activity.

11 High Street
Silverton
Gloucester
GL2 9VL
1 February 20–

Mr T. White
PE Instructor
Silverton Grammar School
Gloucester
GL2 7PT

Dear Mr White

My son Gregory has recently been off school with a severe chest infection and the doctor has advised that he should avoid being outside in cold weather for the next few days. So I would be grateful if you could excuse him from the cross-country run this afternoon.

Yours sincerely

Georgia Hammond (Mrs)

Complaining about bullying in school

2 School Lane
Beauly
Inverness
IV4 9NB
27 February 20–

Mr P. Bowlson
Head Teacher
Highfield School
Dean Road
Beauly
Inverness
IV4 1SD

Dear Mr Bowlson

I wish to inform you of a very serious situation involving our daughter Susan. It appears she has been the victim of a group of older girls who pick on the most junior pupils and demand money from them. When my daughter refused to hand over the small amount of money she had, she was verbally abused, punched and kicked.

Susan is not the sort of child to tell tales and normally looks after herself, but this does seem to be a particularly nasty form of bullying. She does not know the names of the girls involved except for one, Karen Wilcox, who appears to be the ringleader.

As today is Friday, I am keeping Susan at home. She is still very upset, and has some visible bruises. I shall telephone you on Monday morning when you will have received this letter. I hope that you will be able to assure me that this unacceptable behaviour will be stopped immediately and the culprits punished in an appropriate manner.

Yours sincerely

Carol Campbell

Removing a child from school

19 Hazel Street
Grazeley
Wiltshire
CH14 5TF
16 October 20–

Miss M. Metcalfe
Head Teacher
Hampton Park School
Grazeley
Wiltshire
CH14 3RR

Dear Miss Metcalfe

I wish to inform you that our daughter Rachel will be leaving Hampton Park at the end of this term.

My husband's company has relocated to Berkshire and Rachel will be attending Middle Hill School, just outside Newbury, which I understand has an excellent academic record.

Thank you for all the encouragement you and your staff have given to Rachel over the last two years.

Yours sincerely

Elizabeth Walters (Mrs)

26 Mount Court
The Warren
Lythcote Hill
Lincolnshire
LH8 6NU
25 May 20—

Mr P. Smythe
Lythcote School
1 The Hill
Lythcote Hill
Lincolnshire
LH8 6WG

Dear Mr Smythe

My son Peter is in Year 2 in Miss Walker's class.

Although he is trying very hard, he does not seem to be making progress with his reading and he is beginning to find this upsetting as he feels everyone else is 'better' than he is. I have mentioned this to Miss Walker. She reassured us that all the children learn at their own pace, but I am anxious about Peter's reaction to his slow progress and do not want this to become an issue.

I would appreciate it if we could arrange a meeting to discuss how we can best support and encourage Peter, as we would really benefit from your professional advice.

I look forward to hearing from you.

Yours sincerely

Mary and Simon Bowles

Caring for the elderly

As our population ages, many of us will be helping to care for elderly relatives. You may need to write on their behalf, or investigate additional support and help for them either at home or in nursing care.

Enquiry to a care home for the elderly

Mayfields
River Lane
Salisbury
Wiltshire
S23 4WN
6 February 20–

The Manager
The Parks Residential Home
Rotherham
South Yorkshire
S14 3GT

Dear Sir/Madam

My mother is at present in her own home in Rotherham, but has recently begun to find it very difficult to cope on her own. I have therefore been looking around the area for a residential home that she could probably move into. I did think of moving her down here to be closer to me, but she would miss her friends who hopefully would still be able to visit her at the home.

Your facilities have been highly recommended to me and I wonder if you could let me know if there are any vacancies. Please would you also send me a brochure, if one is available. Would the family be responsible for all the fees, or does the local authority pay a proportion of them?

Incidentally, one of my mother's old friends, Barbara Fletcher, is already a resident in your home, which would be a help in settling her in.

Yours faithfully

Penny Appleton

Confirmation of acceptance of a place in a residential home

Mayfields
River Lane
Salisbury
Wiltshire
S23 4WN
6 February 20–

Mrs Walford
The Manager
The Parks Residential Home
Rotherham
South Yorkshire
S14 3GT

Dear Mrs Walford

Thank you very much for your offer of a place in The Parks. As you know, we were very impressed with the facilities when we visited last week, and my mother is excited about moving in. She particularly liked the room you offered her because of its views of the river and woodland. So I am confirming that we will accept your offer and that she will be moving in next Sunday.

Yours sincerely

Penny Appleton

Applying for a place in warden-assisted flats

71 Hill Crescent
Grandford
Cambridgeshire
CM34 4HB
1 July 20–

The Housing Department
Grandford City Council
Council Offices
Grandford
Cambridgeshire
CM34 1TB

Dear Sirs

I write to ask you if there are any flats vacant in sheltered housing estates in Grandford.

These days, my parents are finding it more difficult to cope in their small terraced house with its steep staircase. The garden is also too much for them now. They would prefer a ground-floor flat, with perhaps a small garden attached where they could sit out in the summer. They are perfectly capable of looking after themselves generally, so do not need residential care. But it would be reassuring for me to know that there is someone close by whom they can contact in an emergency.

Please let me know if you have any suitable accommodation.

Yours faithfully

Pamela Anderson (Mrs)

Asking for additional in-home support

26 Mill Road
Shepton
County Antrim
BT41 7DU
15 June 20—

Mrs D. Bennett
Social Services Department
Council Offices
6 Wycombe Close
Shepton
County Antrim
BT18 6DK

Dear Mrs Bennett

My mother is now 84 years of age and is living on her own at 48 Shelley Court, Poundford, County Antrim BT41 7VF. She is now unable to manage regular housework, and I am writing on her behalf to enquire if you are able to offer any help in this area. If you could send me any information on what is available and how we apply, I would be most grateful.

I look forward to hearing from you.

Yours sincerely

Mrs Sarah Malone

96 Willow Road
Tretherne
Cornwall
TR7 6HK
19 April 20—

Mr B. Gibbs
Gibbs, Walker & Sturgeon
456 High Street
Truro
Cornwall
TR8 7HL

Dear Mr Gibbs

I am enquiring about setting up power of attorney for my elderly mother. I would be most grateful if you would send me some information on the subject so that I can find out what is involved. Could you also outline your fee structure. I would then like to make an appointment with you to discuss what action we need to take.

I look forward to hearing from you.

Yours sincerely

Mr Leigh Housego

Wills

Writing a will can be a tricky topic for many people. The following letters will help to raise and resolve issues related to this delicate but important subject.

Asking a friend to be executor of a will

Naturally, it is advisable to ask someone who is likely to be alive and well when you die.

54 Blackhorse Avenue
Cottenham
Cambridgeshire
CA6 2NR
8 May 20–

Dear Albert

I want to ask a favour and I sincerely hope you will be able to help me out.

I am about to make my will. I think you would be well qualified to perform the role of executor, so I'd be really grateful if you could act as one of mine. I have asked my solicitor to be the other one.

Please give the matter some thought anyway. I know it is a thankless task, but if you said yes it would go a long way towards putting my mind at rest.

Yours sincerely,

Seth Watson

8 Maytree Avenue
Happyacre
Northumberland
BT2 9NY
8 July 20–

Dear Janine

I am in the process of making my will and I'm looking for someone to name as guardian for Toby and Lizzie in the event of my death before they reach maturity. There is no doubt that you are the adult that they know and love best apart from us, and if both John and I died when they were still in their teens, you would be the ideal person to look after their interests. Of course, they should have enough money to live on while they're still at school so there would be no financial commitment for you.

Please let me know if you would agree to this.

Love Philippa

Accepting the role of executor

38 Cantrell Avenue
Sidford
Surrey
SD2 9NY
16 May 20–

Dear Seth

It would be an honour for me to act as your executor. I really didn't have to think about it long! Anyway, you can just relax about that side of things now. I'm sure you don't really want to be thinking about dying when you're still so fit and healthy, but I know we all have to make these preparations.

Yours sincerely

Albert

38 Cantrell Avenue
Sidford
Surrey
SD2 9NY
16 May 20–

Dear Seth

I'm really sorry, but I don't feel capable of taking on the executor role. I have no financial expertise whatsoever, and don't feel I could really do the job well enough. I'm also not that young and it's quite likely that I'll die before you do.

Sorry to have to let you down like this, but I wouldn't feel comfortable if you named me as executor.

Yours sincerely

Albert

Asking for review of a will

53 Park Drive
Ripley
Oxfordshire
OX5 9XR
27 March 20–

Messrs Banks and Heartfield
Solicitors
23 Wimbledon Avenue
Oxford
OX5 2QS

Dear Sirs

I am writing to you to ask you if I can review my will made under your guidance 12 years ago. I am recently divorced, and I would therefore like to change some of the contents of the will because my ex-husband should no longer be a beneficiary.

Please can you arrange for someone to go through the will with me in view of the new situation that I find myself in.

Yours faithfully

Michelle Collins

Illness and bereavement

Writing a letter of sympathy is not an easy task. It is preferable to keep any such letters short and make sure that the tone is supportive and appropriate to your relationship with the person concerned.

Sympathy and offer of help in a case of illness

54 Bowden Lane
Charlton
London
SE7 9DU
8 February 20—

Dear Maria

We are extremely sorry to hear that Ian is very ill, and we do hope that you will soon have some better news to report.

Is there any way in which we can help? At times like this, it is often hard to manage, so if there is anything we can do, please don't hesitate to let us know.

Would you like Tom to come here for a few days, as he is so young and must be taking up a great deal of your time? He would be quite happy with James and we would be delighted to have him.

With every sympathy,

Yours sincerely

Margaret and Philip

Avondale
Berkshire Drive
Warrington
Cheshire
WA2 1JW
15 September 20–

Dear Arnold

I was so surprised to hear yesterday that you were in hospital, and have had an operation. I'm sorry that the fates have been unkind to you and I hope that it will not be long before you are back at home.

I don't know much about hospitals, but if anyone can find them amusing, I am sure you can. You have always had the knack of seeing the funny side of a situation, and I guess you'll do it this time. And leave the nurses alone – they have a job to do!

I hope it's okay if I come in and see you some time. I'd really like to.

Best of luck,

Yours ever

Derek

19 Trehurst Crescent
Buxton
Derbyshire
DE17 2NJ
6 November 20–

Dear Mrs Mackay

I have only just heard that you are laid up and under medical supervision. I don't know you very well, but I would be very pleased to help you in any way I can.

Would you like me to come in to be with you one afternoon? Perhaps I could do a few things to help your husband, and it would be a change for you, anyway. There might be other ways in which I could be useful while you are ill. Just let me know.

Hoping you will soon recover,

Yours sincerely

Martha Brown

69 Fursewood Gardens
Lincoln
LN1 9FD
10 May 20–

Dear Aunt Laura

I am sure you will be very sorry to hear that Mum died last night.
The end was peaceful.

I'll write to you again later, when we have made the arrangements for
the funeral.

Yours with love

Katherine

Condolence on a death

The recipient will receive many letters like this, and there is no need
to say a great deal. The main comfort is in feeling the support of
other people at a difficult time.

39 Fircroft Road
Blackheath
London
SE3 2BR
8 February 20–

Dear Mr Gregory

I have just heard of the sad death of your wife.

Margaret and I would like to say how deeply sorry we are. We both
had a great admiration for Mrs Gregory and she will be much missed
by many people.

I cannot tell you how much I feel for you at this time.

In deepest sympathy,

Yours sincerely

Edgar Billing

78 Drury Hill
Nottingham
NG1 4GX
11 May 20–

Dearest Katherine

I am very distressed to hear of your mother's death and I hope you are coping in the sad circumstances.

I know you were always so close to your mother, so her passing away must be particularly difficult for you. Please call me if you want to talk about it, or if you would like to meet up somewhere.

I am so sorry.

Love Laura

Notifying the time of a funeral

73 Westingford Street
London
NW8 2QN
8 January 20–

H. Young Esq
3 Station Avenue
London
NW5 2LF

Dear Mr Young

I have been asked by Miss Yeoman to inform you that the funeral of her father will take place on Tuesday, 11 January, at Holy Trinity Church, Exford Street, London NW8 4XP, at 1.30pm.

Yours sincerely

S. Chang

3 Jedburgh Road
Richmond
Surrey
RD2 9LV
3 April 20–

Dear Mr Pinckney

I am sure you will be sorry to hear that my father died last night. He was in good health until about a week ago, but then he suddenly became ill.

I see from his papers that he had appointed you as one of the executors of his will. I would be most grateful if you could contact me to discuss this matter as soon as is convenient to you.

Yours sincerely

Marjorie Ellam

Formal thanks for sympathies following a death

Printed cards are available for this purpose, but computers and word processors make the printing of several letters with the same message very easy. You could also make the letter more personal by beginning with a conventional salutation, amending the wording slightly and signing it as normal.

69 Truscott Avenue
Burlington
Wolverhampton
W15 5XN
14 June 20–

Mr and Mrs Ackroyd and family gratefully acknowledge your kind expression of sympathy in their sad loss and would like to thank you.

Invitations and replies 4

At one time, most invitations were very formal, but today the balance has shifted, and the formal invitation is now becoming rarer. It is possible to buy printed invitations of various types, with spaces to fill in your name and the person you are inviting, but word processing software has made it simple for most people to produce similar items at home.

When sending an invitation, make sure you include all the information necessary, including date, time and location, dress code (if any) and cost (if relevant). It may also be important to include directions to the place where the event is located, train or bus options and overnight accommodation possibilities. In most situations you will need to know how many people are coming, so do not forget to put the magic initials RSVP at the end of the invitation. It is generally thought correct to reply immediately, but in case you are worried that the recipient will not do so, add a date after the RSVP by which you need replies. Alternatively, you can simply put 'Please reply by *date*'. Replies to formal invitations should follow the style of the invitation closely and repeat the information it contains, so that any misunderstandings about time, date or place can be brought to light.

Here are some examples of invitations, and possible replies.

Parties and celebrations, both formal and informal

Not too long ago, it was quite common for people to send formal invitations to dinner, but this practice has largely died out now. Such invitations are normally by telephone or e-mail or even casually when meeting somebody in the street, and the concept of a formal dinner really only applies to events held by clubs and societies.

Formal and informal invitations for many other occasions and celebrations are still often sent by printed card or letter, although e-mail is sometimes used, and the form can be the same for a posted invitation. See the section on e-mail for the most appropriate uses of this medium of communication (see page 247).

Formal invitation to a dance

The invitation should be printed, with the names of those invited written by hand.

Mr and Mrs A. E. Clarke

request the pleasure of the company of

Mr and Mrs James Stoneham

on Saturday, 4 December 20–

The Horns
Chertsey Vale
Surrey   Dancing 9.30pm–2.30am
ST9 8EU   RSVP

Accepting formal invitation to a dance

The Hollyhocks
Chertsey Vale
Surrey
ST9 8TP
26 November 20–

Mr and Mrs James Stoneham wish to thank Mr and Mrs A. E. Clarke for their kind invitation for 4 December and have much pleasure in accepting.

Declining formal invitation to a dance

The Hollyhocks
Chertsey Vale
Surrey
ST9 8TP
26 November 20–

Mr and Mrs James Stoneham wish to thank Mr and Mrs A. E. Clarke for their kind invitation for 4 December. It is with much regret that they have to decline because of a prior engagement.

Invitation for Christmas drinks

John and Angela Hickling
request the pleasure of
the company of

Stefan Kusznierz

on Sunday, 22 December 20–, between 6 and 8pm
for pre-Christmas drinks and nibbles

RSVP
5 Ranelagh Gardens
Markfield
Northumberland
NE34 4PP

Mr and Mrs Arthur Wilmshurst
request the pleasure of
the company of

James Arbuthnot

at the coming of age party
for their son Tom
at Milton St Percy Community Centre
on Saturday, 3 April 20–, at 8pm

RSVP
23 Waggoners Walk
Milton St Percy
Gloucester
GL5 4TY

Acceptance of 18th birthday party invitation

The Manse
Holbeck Drive
Balston
Gloucestershire
GL15 7TY
12 March 20–

Mr James Arbuthnot wishes to thank Mr and Mrs Arthur Wilmshurst
for their kind invitation to the coming of age party for their son, Tom,
on 3 April 20–, which he has much pleasure in accepting.

Declining an 18th birthday party invitation

The Manse
Holbeck Drive
Balston
Gloucester
GL15 7TY
12 March 20–

Mr James Arbuthnot wishes to thank Mr and Mrs Arthur Wilmshurst
for their kind invitation to the coming of age party for their son Tom
on 3 April 20–, but unfortunately he is unable to accept, because of a
prior engagement.

Informal invitation to dinner

5 Tyburn Gardens
Caldecott
Leicestershire
LE15 4RT
4 May 20–

Hi John and Sue

We're having a few people over for dinner on 17 May, about 8pm, and wonder if you'd like to come. I know it's a bit of a trek for you, but we could find you a place to stay locally afterwards if that'd help. Then you could both drink!

Please let us know, as we want to know how many to cook for.

All the best

Rod and Barry

Accepting an informal invitation to dinner

12 Glebe Close
Hickling
Nottinghamshire
NG18 4RN
6 May 20–

Nice one, Rod and Barry! We'd love to come. Will George and Sandy be there? Don't worry about accommodation. Sue and I can just crash out in the back of the 4X4. It shouldn't be too cold, and if it is, we probably won't notice!

See you on the 17th!

Best wishes

John

12 Glebe Close
Hickling
Nottinghamshire
NG18 4RN
6 May 20–

It's a real shame, Rod and Barry, but we can't make it on the 17th. Sue's invited her parents down that weekend (don't worry, I can cope!) and it's a bit late to cancel them now.

As we can't see you then, would you like to come up here the following weekend, or any other weekend after that until about the end of June?

Look forward to hearing from you,

Best wishes

John

Invitation to a children's party

17 Burnside Avenue
South Ham
Essex
HA5 2JB
12 December 20–

Dear Mrs Singh

Daisy and Charles are having a party on Tuesday, 3 January from 4.30 to 7.30pm in the Scout Hut and they would like to invite Jaswinder. It's Daisy's birthday that day and Charles's a week later.

If you are coming to fetch him yourself afterwards, you could come a little earlier than 7.30 to see some of the fun. We have a magician booked for 6.30.

I hope Jaswinder will be able to come, and it would be nice to meet you as well.

Yours sincerely

Mary Seymour

Accepting an invitation to a children's party

24 Bilston Avenue
South Ham
Essex
HA5 2AA
22 December 20–

Dear Mrs Seymour

Thank you very much for inviting Jaswinder to your children's party on 3 January. He is very excited and is looking forward to coming.

I will come at 6.30 as you suggest. Jaswinder is fascinated by magicians, and I'm sure I will enjoy the show, too!

Looking forward to seeing you,

Yours sincerely

Mrs A. Singh

Declining an invitation to a children's party

24 Bilston Avenue
South Ham
Essex
HA5 2JB
22 December 20–

Dear Mrs Seymour

Jaswinder is most upset, but he will not be able to accept the invitation for the party on 3 January. We will be away with relatives in Oxford that weekend.

Please thank Daisy and Charles and tell them how sorry Jaswinder is that he will not be able to come. He is looking forward to seeing Charles at school on the 5th.

It was very nice of you to ask him.

Yours sincerely

Mrs A. Singh

Weddings

Wedding stationery is big business, so it is quite likely that if you are planning a wedding you may be buying what you need. However, with a little time, a word processor and some quality paper or card, you may wish to do the job yourself.

Formal invitation to a wedding

The invitation should be printed, with the names of those invited written by hand.

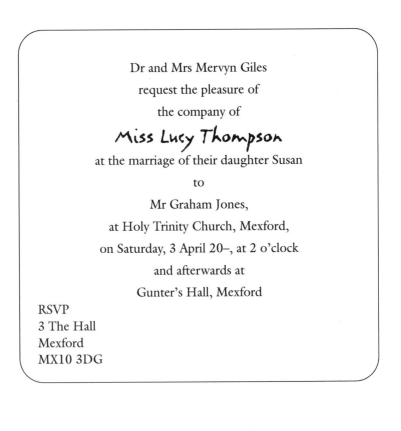

Dr and Mrs Mervyn Giles

request the pleasure of

the company of

Miss Lucy Thompson

at the marriage of their daughter Susan

to

Mr Graham Jones,

at Holy Trinity Church, Mexford,

on Saturday, 3 April 20–, at 2 o'clock

and afterwards at

Gunter's Hall, Mexford

RSVP
3 The Hall
Mexford
MX10 3DG

The invitation should be printed, with the names of those invited written by hand.

Mr James B. Warren and Mrs Gillian Fisher

request the pleasure of

the company of

Mr Adam Wells

at the marriage of their daughter, Pamela,

to

Mr Percival Jones,

at St Lawrence's Church, Grimley,

on Saturday, 15 July 20–, at 2.30pm

and afterwards at

The Grange, Upstead

RSVP
Mrs Gillian Fisher
23 Forster Street
Upstead
RT45 4RT

Reply to a formal wedding invitation

The Red Roofs
Mexford
Lancashire
MX2 9BD
20 February 20–

Miss Lucy Thompson thanks Dr and Mrs Mervyn Giles for their kind invitation to be present at the wedding of their daughter Susan to Mr Graham Jones. She has much pleasure in accepting.

The Doves
Eckford
Kent
EK10 4XZ
3 April 20–

Dear Bill

You might be surprised to hear that June and I have decided to tie the knot at last.

We're getting married at Sittingbourne Register Office on 23 May at 2 o'clock and having a party afterwards at June's parents' place. We'd very much like it if you could come to both. I enclose a couple of maps to help you find the Register Office and June's parents' house.

Let us know if you are coming, because we need to know how many to cater for!

All the best

Ronald

This is a relatively new addition to the list of ceremonies, so there is little precedent for the type of invitation. However, there is no reason why it should not follow a similar style to that of a formal wedding invitation. Even in an age of increased equality between the sexes, tradition dictates that a wedding celebration is generally organised by the bride's parents, so some adjustment to the wording may be inevitable, probably to include both sets of parents. Perhaps more likely is that the invitation will be from the couple themselves.

Jim Albright and Caspar Stonesby

request the pleasure of

the company of

Mr Radojko Milosevic

at their civil partnership ceremony

at

at Ambleford Register Office

on Saturday, 14 September 20–, at 12 o'clock

and afterwards at

The Blue Boar, Ambleford

RSVP
40 Chilwell Road
Ambleford
RS45 1QW

Christenings and other celebrations

A christening, or any naming ceremony, is an opportunity to gather friends and family to celebrate the entry of a newcomer to the family or community. It is often the occasion for a family party as well as a religious ceremony.

Invitation to a christening

38 Pope's Drive
Bankford
Durham
D23 4NH
2 April 20–

Dear Jo

David is to be christened at St Paul's Church, Bankford, at 2.30pm on Sunday, 5 May and Will and I would be delighted if you could be there. We'll be having a little party to celebrate at the nearby Bull's Head afterwards.

Will sends his best wishes.

Yours sincerely

Rhiannon

Accepting an invitation to a christening

40 Byron's Avenue
Bankford
Durham
D23 6NB
9 April 20–

Dear Rhiannon

Thank you for the invitation to David's christening – the first of life's milestones! I'd love to come, and I'm looking forward to seeing you and Will, as well as little David, of course.

See you in church on 5 May.

Yours sincerely

Jo

Holidays and outings

You may feel that discussing this with someone is the best way to make arrangements for outings, but on occasion, sending someone a letter allows them time to think about the arrangements and decide if they would like to follow up on your offer.

Inviting a friend to stay

Cranford
Middle Haven
Devon
MH19 4XP
3 August 20–

Dear Françoise

I heard from Mum the other day that she saw you in Loughborough, and it made me feel so guilty that we'd not been in touch with you since we moved down here. The sea air is doing us all good, and Mick's new job couldn't be better. I've started working hard on my pottery, and hope to be marketing some of my wares soon.

But my point in writing is to ask if you will come and stay with us for a few days or even a week. We have plenty of room, and I'm free to take time off whenever I like, of course. In fact, I won't ask, I'll just say that you have to come! Any time you're free over the next few weeks or months. We don't really have anything planned. Probably best to make it before the winter, though, unless you like walking along a beach when the sea is rough (which I admit I do rather enjoy).

Drop me a line saying when you can come. Mick will be extremely put out if you say you can't! If you think we're putting pressure on you, you're right!

Love

Janet

5 Trelawny Terrace
Burton on the Wolds
Loughborough
Leicestershire
LE20 4EE
10 August 20–

Dear Janet

I was really delighted to receive your letter. You're very kind to think of me and to ask me to stay. Despite what you say, you must be very busy, not only with work, but also getting the house sorted out.

I must say I feel the need for a break by the sea, and to be with you and Mick would make it really special. So I'd be glad to come and spend some time with you. I think I'd like to come while it's still fairly warm, although I know that's never guaranteed in this country, so could we make it towards the end of this month or in September some time? I could stay for a week, if you're sure you can cope with me for that long!

Could you pick me up from the station? I think the trains go to Plymouth and Exeter, but I don't know which is nearest to you.

Love Françoise

Declining an invitation to stay

5 Trelawny Terrace
Burton on the Wolds
Loughborough
Leicestershire
LE20 4EE
10 August 20–

Dear Janet

I was really delighted to receive your letter, but I'm so sorry, I won't be able to come and stay, not for a while, anyway. I'm under real pressure at work, on a particular project that we have to finish by Christmas. Perhaps I'll have some time off in the New Year, but I'm not sure at the moment. You're very kind to think of me and to ask me to come. Despite what you say, you must be very busy, not only with work, but also getting the house sorted out.

I must say it would be good to have a break by the sea, and to be with you and Mick would make it really special. Can I write again when I know what's happening at work? Also, could you pick me up from the station? I think the trains go to Plymouth and Exeter, but I don't know which is nearest to you. I'd rather not drive that far, not in my car anyway!

Love Françoise

Inviting a friend for a holiday

The Grey Towers
Littlebourne
Kent
LB10 9DX
1 April 20–

Dear Helen

We're planning our annual holiday and wonder if you'd like to come with us. There's nobody we'd like better to spend the time with, and I know things have been difficult for you recently, so you probably need a break.

We were thinking of going to Austria in July by car. Marco is very proud of his new Mercedes, but he'd be happy to let either of us chauffeur him for a few miles every so often. It had better not be too often though, or he'll start to expect it! If you don't like driving on the right-hand side of the road, don't worry, we're not going to force you. The most important thing is that you are able to relax for a bit. We certainly intend to make it a relaxing holiday, and we're not going to spend too much time seeing the sights once we've reached our destination, probably in the Tyrol somewhere.

Please say you will come. It's early days yet, and we're still studying brochures. Would you like to come round one evening to have a look at them? Perhaps you know more about Austria than we do.

Yours with love

Christine

Middle Cloisters
Canterbury
CA4 5DP
7 April 20–

Dear Christine

You can't know how much I appreciate your offer. I accept! I did go to Austria once in my youth, but I don't remember much about it. I have driven on the right fairly recently, on holiday in Spain two years ago, and it doesn't faze me at all. I just hope that Marco will trust me with his Mercedes!

I could come over any day during the week, apart from Wednesday. How about next week some time?

Yours, filled with anticipation

Helen

Middle Cloisters
Canterbury
CA4 5DP
7 April 20–

Dear Christine

Thank you so much for thinking of me, but I'm going to have to say no this time. I still need to sort everything out, and until I do, I won't be able to relax anywhere. I hope you will understand. It's certainly not because I don't like the thought of a holiday with you and Marco. I really do, but perhaps next year would be better.

Love Helen

Around the home 5

Sometimes the quality of your letter writing can affect the kind of service you get from companies and organisations that supply your everyday needs. This chapter contains appropriate letters dealing with matters of concern to a householder.

Utilities and suppliers

It can be hard to strike up any communication with a utility company and it might take some persistence to get the result you want. The best approach is to be polite and businesslike.

Querying a household account

This can be adapted depending on the organisation involved.

84 Brownlow Gardens
Easterly
Cumbria
EY3 4TJ
4 January 20–

The General & District Gas Co. plc
23 High Street
Easterly
Cumbria
EY1 4ND

Dear Sirs

On receiving your account for the last quarter's supply of gas, I was amazed to see how large the bill was.

As the consumption indicated is far greater than in any previous quarter and as there is no reason for supposing that we have used more gas, I can only conclude that the meter is not functioning correctly. Could you please check this as soon as possible?

Yours faithfully

S. McDonald

84 Brownlow Gardens
Easterly
Cumbria
EY3 4TJ
4 January 20–

Your ref: Sanjay Patel
Acme Gas Company plc
Gas House
Easterly
Cumbria
EY1 1TA

Dear Sirs

Following our telephone conversation today, I have decided that I would like to change gas supplier from the General and District Gas Co. plc to yourselves. I have been very dissatisfied with the service from the General and District and trust that the service you provide will be a distinct improvement.

Please let me know if I need to inform the General and District of the change myself, or whether you will do this for me.

Yours faithfully

S. McDonald

Request to cancel newspapers for the period of an annual holiday

26 Travis Close
Bilton
Somerset
TN34 5RF

Armstrong and Whitworth
High Street
Bilton
Somerset
TN34 5TY

Dear Sirs

Please could you cancel my newspapers for the fortnight 7–20 August inclusive, and resume normal deliveries on 21 August.

Thank you.

Yours faithfully

Mark Williams

This is in response to an advertisement in a newspaper. The reference Dept DM 15 appeared in the advertisement.

16 Halifax Street
Canterbury
Kent
CT6 8NM
19 November 20–

Castle Flooring Ltd
Dept DM 15
Queen Mary's Road
London
NW6 3KT

Dear Sirs

Please send me a free sample of your 'No Waste' floor covering. I enclose a stamped, self-addressed envelope.

Yours faithfully

N. Chatterton

Enc

Advertisements in newspapers selling direct to the public often give the option only of buying online or by telephone. For goods for sale by post, there is sometimes a form to cut out and fill in, but if not, or if you prefer not to cut up your new magazine, here is a letter you could use.

634 Crescent Road
Shotley Bridge
County Durham
DH13 4RT
18 July 20–

Messrs Berry and Berry Ltd
Bargain Department
High Street
Winchester
Hampshire
SO23 2YL

Dear Sirs

In The Spectator dated 23 July 20– you advertise overalls, Item No. 457700, at £15.50.

Please send me two sets, one in blue and one in green, both 46 in. in length.

I enclose my cheque for £34 to include the cost of postage.

Yours faithfully

Annie Turnbury (Mrs)

39 The Broadway
Trelford
Grandford
Cambridgeshire
CA12 2VU
10 June 20–

Council Services Department
Grandford City Council
Council Offices
Grandford
Cambridgeshire
CM34 1TB

Dear Sirs

<u>Refuse Collection</u>

I wish to complain about the level of service we are getting from you. For the second time in a month our normal waste bin has not be emptied on a Tuesday, despite the fact that it has been put outside our house in clear view and before 7am, as instructed.

Now that our normal bin is only collected fortnightly and the recycling bin every other week, this places us in a very awkward position. We have no other bin in which to put rubbish and we have found that leaving it by the bin in plastic sacks is no solution, as they are attacked by cats and wild animals such as foxes.

Under the circumstances, and considering the possible health risks of rubbish accumulating by our property, I think you should arrange a special journey to collect our rubbish.

I look forward to a speedy resolution of this problem.

Yours faithfully

H. R. Woodward

Maintenance and repairs

Although many repairs are arranged by telephone, it is useful to put the details in writing, particularly where sums of money are involved, to avoid problems when it comes to paying your bill.

29 Churchill Drive
Rotherton
North Yorkshire
RH19 6BD
19 September 20–

Alldays & Brown Ltd
Baldwin Street
Maidsgrove
North Yorkshire
RH9 6EU

Dear Sirs

We are considering having repairs done to our property at the above address. As far as we can see, the work will roughly be:

1 Demolition of existing front porch

2 Replacement of porch with a new brick structure of similar design

3 Removal of all rubble and rubbish

We would be grateful if you could arrange to give us an estimate. You could come and examine the buildings on any weekday between 10am and 5pm. Please telephone me on 01234 567890 so that we can arrange a convenient time.

Yours faithfully

Derwent Morgan

17 Hillside Lane
Lincoln
LN3 9YG
21 September 20–

R. S. Bland (Plumbers)
4 Dover Street
Lincoln
LN4 6DG

Dear Sirs

You installed our central heating boiler two years ago, and it is now time for its regular service. Please give me a call on 01234 567890 to arrange this. I realise this is a busy time of year for you, but any time on weekdays or at weekends would be possible.

I look forward to hearing from you.

Yours faithfully

A. Barkworth

Accepting an estimate

28 Barnfield Close
Brackley
Lancashire
LN3 8NM
7 October 20–

Your ref: SW 63/GW

Messrs Stokely and Wicks (Builders) Ltd
46 Winlow Lane
Brackley
Lancs
LN3 1ST

Dear Sirs

This letter is to confirm our acceptance of your estimate dated 4 October 20– for building repairs at the above address. We also confirm that a start date of 3 November is acceptable and look forward to seeing you at 9am on that date.

Yours faithfully

George Wills

28 Barnfield Close
Brackley
Lancashire
LN3 8NM
7 October 20–

Your ref: SW 63/GW

Messrs Stokely and Wicks (Builders) Ltd
46 Winlow Lane
Brackley
Lancs
LN3 1ST

Dear Sirs

Thank you for your estimate.

Unfortunately, it is a little more than we can afford at the moment. I wonder if there is any way it could be reduced, by using cheaper materials, for example, or perhaps by postponing some of the less urgent work.

Please advise.

Yours faithfully

George Wills

28 Barnfield Close
Brackley
Lancashire
LN3 8NM
17 November 20–

Messrs Stokely and Wicks (Builders) Ltd
46 Winlow Lane
Brackley
Lancs
LN3 1ST

Dear Sirs

As you know, you recently completed repairs to our property.

Unfortunately, we are not happy with the state of the building after the work. Some of the brickwork and pointing is of very poor standard, and it is really unacceptable to leave rubble on our vegetable plot.

Until these issues are dealt with, I shall withhold final payment of your account.

Yours faithfully

George Wills

Problems and complaints

Sometimes the only way to get a problem resolved is to keep writing until you are satisfied. Keep copies of all correspondence in case of further dispute.

Returning faulty goods

When returning goods by post, always keep a photocopy of the receipt and obtain proof of postage.

68 Round Lane
Boundary Road
Heathfield
Sussex
HA4 5DT
30 June 20–

Your ref: Mrs Janet Osborne

Messrs Beadmore & Long
10 Friar Street
Barrowden
BD2 9XP

Dear Sirs

Following a telephone conversation with Mrs Osborne this morning, I'm returning the handbag that I recently bought in your shop, together with the receipt.

As I told Mrs Osborne, I had only been using the handbag for a couple of days, and the handle came off. It was a tricky situation, because it meant that the bag dropped to the ground in a busy street and could easily have been stolen. Fortunately, this did not happen, but I still feel I should have my money back because this is supposedly high-quality merchandise and should have lasted for many years.

I look forward to receiving a full refund and I trust that you will also reimburse me for my postage.

Yours faithfully

A. B. Mitchell (Mrs)

12 Stokes Close
Armley
Manchester
MA3 8NM
13 March 20–

Customer Services
Superfast Train Company plc
The Sidings
Grandford
Cambridgeshire
CM1 12RT

Dear Sirs

I wish to claim a refund for a train journey that I was unable to make because of a strike by train drivers on 11 March this year. I enclose the ticket and a copy of the credit card receipt. Please refund my credit card account.

Thank you.

Yours faithfully

Gunther Sonntag

12 Hill Rise
Streetley
Grandford
Cambridgeshire
BA13 8PP
7 February 20–

Customer Services
Superfast Train Company plc
The Sidings
Grandford
Cambridgeshire
CM1 12RT

Dear Sirs

I am writing to complain about the poor quality of your commuter services. On a number of occasions recently my morning train has been either cancelled or heavily delayed. As a result, I have missed some important business meetings. In addition, the level of cleanliness and tidiness of the trains themselves is appalling.

Under the circumstances, I feel that I deserve some compensation. I am a season ticket holder, and deserve better service, especially in view of the extraordinary increase in the price you introduced in January, which was well above the rate of inflation.

Yours faithfully

Arthur Timms

17 Seaview Road
Copley
East Sussex
BN1 7FD
19 February 20–

The Environmental Health Officer
Copley Borough Council
High Street
Copley
East Sussex
BN3 4PP

Dear Sir

I wish to complain about the early start being made by builders working on the flats in Spelthorne Park Road, which is just a few metres from the back of our house.

For the last few days, work has commenced as early as 5am. I am sure you will agree that such an early start cannot be permitted as it is impossible to sleep once work has begun.

I would be most grateful if you could look into this as soon as possible and inform me of what action you will be taking.

Yours faithfully

S. J. Carter

Tact and diplomacy are very important here. You need to make sure a minor complaint does not escalate into a full-blown 'neighbours from hell' scenario. This sample letter contains an offer to help in dealing with an issue of concern, which lessens the sense of confrontation.

36 Ford Lane
Ferryford
Powys
SY17 2BG
8 July 20–

Dear Mr Henslowe

I am sorry to have to appear unneighbourly, but your dog has recently been causing a lot of damage to my garden. It has ruined quite a number of plants and has also spoilt the appearance of the flower beds.

The main reason this has happened is the poor state of the fences between your garden and mine. I would gladly effect repairs to the fences, but they are your responsibility and so I would have to charge you for doing this.

Please let me know soon if you wish me to repair the fences, so that further damage to my garden can be avoided.

Yours sincerely

Geoff Ripon

38 Burfield Road
Brockford
Cheshire
C8 6FR
1 June 20–

The Chief Planning Officer
Brockford Council
Brockford Town Hall
218–240 Cross Road
Brockford
Cheshire
C8 6FR

Dear Sir

Re: Planning Application Number 179463, 40 Burfield Road, Brockford

I wish to object to the above planning application.

Having viewed the plans, I am sure that this building, if constructed, would block off the light from my downstairs rooms and much of my back garden during the afternoon and evening.

I request that you take this into account when considering this application and suggest that you reject it forthwith.

Yours faithfully

R. Hancock (Ms)

3 Orchard Mews
Nottingham
NG2 9HF
30 August 20–

The Manager
Summer Tours Ltd
27 White Lane
Nottingham
NG3 7XC

Dear Sir

Re: Holiday Ref. H056; Receipt No. A10578

I am writing to complain about the accommodation provided for my wife and me on the above holiday from 11 to 24 August 20–.

I booked the holiday at your offices on 16 February. We were told that we would have an air-conditioned room with balcony and private bathroom. This was confirmed in writing by your Mr Jones on 20 February. However, when we arrived at the hotel on 11 August we were shown to a room that had none of these features. We immediately complained to your courier, Alan Smith, but were told that the hotel had made a mistake over the booking and no other room was available.

The standard of accommodation that we were forced to accept severely affected our enjoyment of the holiday. In light of this, and the fact that your company will have paid less for this room than the one advertised, I therefore expect an appropriate rebate on the sum paid by us.

I look forward to hearing from you and receiving your cheque in the very near future.

Yours faithfully

Robert Brown

39 Grove Drive
Leicester
LE13 5DL
8 September 20–

The Manager
The Cock Hotel
Ambleford
Staffordshire
ST40 5TY

Dear Madam

I spoke to your receptionist about this matter when I checked out this morning after staying one night in your hotel, and she advised me to write to you.

I was assured when I booked the room in May that it would be a quiet room. I needed a good night's sleep before my important meeting with international colleagues at the airport this lunchtime. I was therefore dismayed to be kept awake until after midnight by a karaoke evening taking place in the bar below. When I phoned reception at 11pm, I was given a cursory apology but nothing was done to stop the noise.

I realise that the karaoke evening had probably not been arranged when I booked in May, but I feel you should have kept a note of my request for quietness, and informed me of the situation or transferred me to a room in the annexe.

I look forward to some compensation from you for this extreme inconvenience.

Yours faithfully

S. Gurry

7 The Treeway
Portaton
Somerset
T53 6DU
8 July 20–

Dear Neighbour,

No doubt you will have read in the Evening Gazette of the plans for a wind farm to be built at Portaton.

I am not opposed to wind farms in principle and accept that there might be many potential benefits for the environment as a whole. However, I believe that for one to be established at Portaton would ruin an area of great natural beauty. I am organising a petition that I will be forwarding to the company concerned, with a request that the wind farm is built elsewhere.

I am therefore asking if you would support me by signing this petition. Copies are available at The Royal Oak, Strangeways petrol station and The Cheeky Chippy on Castle Street.

Thank you.

Yours sincerely

Andrew Dutt

Asking for the return of a loaned item

27 Main Street
Branston
Lancashire
PR5 2BG
8 July 20–

Dear Terry

I am going to put up some shelves at the weekend, but I can't find my ratchet screwdriver. I seem to recall that I lent it to you some time ago, but I don't think I have had it back yet.

Could you look it out for me, please? I'll pop round and pick it up on Friday, if that's convenient.

Thanks.

Best wishes

Geoff

7 The Freeway
Portaton
Somerset
T53 6DH
18 July 20–

Charles Tring MP
House of Commons
London
SW1A 0AA

Dear Mr Tring

Re: Proposed wind farm at Portaton airfield

I am writing to you as one of your constituents and also as someone with great experience of environmentalism.

The proposed wind farm at Portaton is an admirable concept, but in completely the wrong place. What is the point of looking after the environment by using renewable energy sources if you then cause damage to the environment by ruining an area of great natural beauty? This is not 'nimbyism', it is simply common sense. A campaign has recently been started to oppose this plan and no doubt protestors will soon make their presence felt. But I feel that there are so many flaws in the arguments of those in favour of the scheme that a word or two with the right people would soon put a stop to it.

Accordingly, I hope you will be able to raise this matter with the appropriate government departments and, if necessary, in the House of Commons.

Yours sincerely

Andrew Dutt
Secretary
The Environmental Action Society

Security issues

Concerns over the safety and security of your home and property should always be raised in a formal and businesslike manner.

Proposing setting up a Neighbourhood Watch Scheme

71 Chilby Road
Heron Fields
West Midlands
B15 2SV
4 October 20–

To all residents of Chilby Road, Grant Avenue
and Norton Vale

Dear Fellow Resident

Neighbourhood Watch

As you will know, the level of crime in this area has risen enormously in the past year. There were six burglaries in September alone, and several instances of vandalism to cars and property.

The burglaries and vandalism are making living here much less attractive than it used to be, and the value of our properties is likely to fall.

I feel we need to set up a Neighbourhood Watch Scheme to help deal with this worrying situation.

Please could you fill in the following form and return it to me if you are interested.

Thank you

Jim Chalmers

- -

To Jim Chalmers
71 Chilby Road
Heron Fields
West Midlands
B15 2SV

I am interested in becoming a member of a Neighbourhood Watch Scheme for the Chilby Road area.

Signed

Address

57 Balance Street
Kettering
Northamptonshire
NN1 2PC
25 May 20–

Community Police Department
Kettering Police Station
Main Street
Kettering
Northamptonshire
NN15 5DI

Dear Sirs

I am writing to express my concerns about the number of people that have been seen loitering in my road.

There are several take-away restaurants in the vicinity and people congregate here, before and after they have bought their food. I am sure that most customers are law-abiding, but there have been several occasions when I have noticed groups of people walking up and down the road in a suspicious manner for up to an hour at a time.

I should be obliged if one of your officers could come along to Balance Street to investigate this situation. It is making me extremely nervous and I am reluctant to leave my home in the evenings.

Yours faithfully

Mrs Laura Bottomley

Bridge Cottage
Station Road
Weston
Hampshire
SO23 8TW
10 November 20–

Seamus Biggins
Claims Department
Carefree Insurance Company
Steady Street
Exeter
Devon
EX10 1SB

Dear Mr Biggins

Policy number CIC10078345

Further to my telephone conversation with you earlier today, I am writing to confirm my claim in respect of damage to my property.

Some time between 8am and 6pm on 9 November, someone entered my back garden and caused a lot of damage. Several plant pots were overturned, some were broken and the contents strewn around. My water butt was emptied, causing damage to the nearby summer house. Also the lock was broken on my potting shed and several bags of compost were emptied over the lawn.

I should be grateful if someone from your company could call as soon as possible to assess this damage, so that my claim may be processed without delay.

Yours sincerely

David Rosenthal

Holidays

Holidays are not supposed to add to your stress, so it is advisable to confirm all bookings in writing.

To a specialist travel agent seeking accommodation

Independent travellers will normally book accommodation direct, but occasionally it may be necessary to use the services of an expert

27 Main Street
Woolmer
Norfolk
N14 5TY
14 January 20–

Ms Evelyn Armitage
45 Upper Way
Ryton
Nr Woolmer
N13 T56

Dear Ms Armitage

I have booked a fortnight at a spa in Mexico in March, but I will be arriving late in Guadalajara on 20 May and need accommodation there for one night before going on to the spa. Could you arrange that for me, please? I would prefer a mid-priced hotel, nothing too fancy but with an adequate level of comfort, and an en suite bathroom.

I look forward to hearing from you.

Yours sincerely

Jack Thompson

Remember, not all hotels have staff who speak English!

4 Southborne Road
Cookham
Berkshire
SL6 2RT
17 August 20–

The Manager
Hotel de la Poste
Villeblanc 1009
Brussels
Belgium

Dear Sir

Thank you for your kind hospitality during our stay at your hotel last week. We very much enjoyed our visit and hope to return some time next year.

Unfortunately, my wife has discovered that she left her walking shoes in Room 304 of the hotel. If they have been found, she would be very grateful to have them returned to her. We would, of course, reimburse you for the costs involved. Perhaps you could find out in advance, and let us know, so that we can send you a credit card payment.

With our best wishes,

Yours faithfully

Alec Green

It is always best to contact a hotel first by telephone or e-mail to ensure that they have a room free. You can then follow up with a confirmation letter and deposit.

15 Mandela Avenue
Kingston
Suffolk
IP45 5YY
12 June 20–

The Manager
Seaview Hotel
Coast Town
Dorset
LM40 5TY

Dear Sir

Following our telephone conversation today, I would like to confirm that I will be taking the family room offered for the week commencing 7 August. I enclose a cheque for £200 as a deposit.

I look forward to seeing you in August.

Yours faithfully

Brad Clooney

45 Sycamore Close
Newtown
Gwynedd
LL40 4GG
12 February 20–

Bradley Holidays
34 Carrington Street
Manchester
M23 5RT

Dear Sirs

I would be grateful if you could send me a few brochures for your all-inclusive holidays in the Mediterranean this summer and autumn. I am particularly interested in Spain and the Greek islands. Thank you.

Yours faithfully

Jonas Treadgold

Financial topics | 6

Financial matters can be very delicate subjects, especially between individuals. The temptation is to beat about the bush, resulting in a lack of clarity. It is actually very important to be clear about what you need to discuss, and therefore to come to the point quickly.

Managing your money

Where money is concerned, it is also best to have matters recorded in writing, for your own security and peace of mind.

Asking a friend for a loan

7 Priory Grove
Nightingale Lane
Palmer's Green
London
N15 2SV
10 June 20–

Dear Hugh

I'm extremely sorry to bother you about such matters, but recent repairs to the house have exhausted my savings and I'm in financial difficulties at the moment. I wonder if you could lend me £500 or so for three or four months. It would see me safely round the corner and be a load off my mind. I have asked my brother William, but with his large family, he has no money to spare and can't help me just now.

If you can't do it, please don't hesitate to say no. But if you can, I'd really appreciate it.

All the best

Colin

Replying to a request for a loan

309 The Broadway
Palmers Green
London
NW15 2VU
15 June 20–

Dear Colin

Don't worry, I've plenty of money to spare at the moment, and I enclose a cheque for £500. It must be quite a strain on you and Doreen. I could even manage a bit more, if it would help. Don't feel obliged to pay it back in three or four months, although I would appreciate having it by the end of the year.

My kind regards to both of you,

Yours

Hugh

309 The Broadway
Palmers Green
London
NW15 2VU
15 June 20—

Dear Colin

Sorry to say things are a bit tight for me too at the moment, and I can't afford to lend you the £500 you asked for. I do have about £100 to spare, and could let you have that for a couple of months, but perhaps it would be better to go to a bank. Or are any of your other friends better off right now?

I'm really sorry to let you down. I hope Doreen's coping all right with the situation. I know very well what it's like when sudden unexpected expenses crop up.

I hope you soon get back on an even keel.

All the best

Hugh

309 The Broadway
Palmers Green
London
NW15 2VU
9 September 20—

Dear Colin

Two or three months ago you were suffering financial difficulties and I lent you £100. I'm sorry to say, I need that money back now. As I said when I lent it to you, things were a bit tight even then and I now have a number of bills that need paying. So please can you let me have the money back this week?

Yours sincerely

Hugh

78 Oakdale Drive
North Cheam
Tyne and Wear
NE8 2ZZ
13 November 20—

Dear Jilly

After our conversation at your uncle's party last week, as promised here are my thoughts on credit cards.

First of all, I should point out that credit cards can be extremely dangerous things. Banks and other credit card companies tend to give people a fairly high credit limit (the total amount of money you can actually spend using your card) and subconsciously you may think that you suddenly have a lot of extra money and you can just go out and spend it. I'm not suggesting for a minute that you're stupid about such things, but there are a lot of intelligent people who've managed to get themselves into serious debt by using a credit card.

Okay, dire warnings over with. Credit cards are also incredibly useful things to have. They mean you don't need to carry lots of cash around with you when you go shopping and you can also buy things online. All you need to do is give the card to the shop assistant, and then key in your PIN number, and you've bought the goods! Keep the receipt and check off the amount on your credit card statement, which comes every month. As long as you pay the whole lot off by the date shown on your statement, the credit card company won't charge you interest for using the card. You need to budget, to know how much money you need to have by that certain date each month so that you can avoid paying interest. If you start paying interest because you don't pay off the entire credit card bill, and you keep using the credit card, then the bill tends to get bigger and bigger, and you may start finding it difficult to pay. If that happens, it's best to pull your horns in a bit, tell your friends you can't go out quite as much during the week, and avoid using the card for a while.

Remember that the credit card company always takes the interest payment before they reduce the money you owe. Don't be distracted by the minimum payment on your bill. If you only pay the minimum you will soon get into higher and higher interest payments!

That's more or less it. If anything puzzles you, please let me know. I've a lot of experience of these things, and I'm always pleased to offer advice.

Love

Andrew

54 Amberley Road
Appleton
Essex
AN3 4DV
31 January 20–

The Secretary
Acme Holdings Ltd
Broadway
Appleton
AN1 9XR

Dear Sir

Recently, you sent me a dividend warrant for £100, in respect of 200 shares that I hold in your company.

Unfortunately the warrant has been destroyed or mislaid. Please inform me whether it is possible to issue a duplicate or, if this cannot be done, what normally happens in such circumstances.

Yours faithfully

K. Brightwell

Banks and financial institutions

Many financial matters can be dealt with quickly and effectively either by phone or online. Nevertheless, if these options are not available, or if you prefer to conduct business affairs in writing, the following templates will be useful.

To a finance company about difficulty with repayments

15 Dower Road
Morvan
Fort William
PH22 9NP
1 July 20–

Southern Leasing
12–14 Arlington Square
London
SW1 6HL

Dear Sirs

Re: Agreement 91837/SDF/986 – Ford Focus

I am having some difficulty in meeting the repayments for the car that I bought last year under the terms of the above hire-purchase agreement. To date, I have paid regularly every month, but I now find that my outgoings are more than I can afford.

I do not wish to default on my debt to your company and would therefore be most grateful if you would consider allowing me to make smaller payments over a longer period.

Please could you let me know if such a change to my existing arrangement is possible and, if so, what terms you are able to offer.

Yours faithfully

Peter Mackieson

55 Church Drive
Church Romford
Cheshire
WA45 5TY
25 February 20–

The Manager
Bank of the Northwest
Warrington
Cheshire
WA1 4RG

Dear Sir

Current Account No 34561234

I am writing to you about the recent deterioration in service from your bank.

I have been a customer of your bank for almost 20 years, and have always had satisfactory service. Recently, however, with the introduction of your new call centre in Penzance, far away from and rather out of touch with the needs of the people of Cheshire, I have been treated very poorly.

First of all, I find the attitude of the 'customer service advisers' very off-hand. I know they are very busy and under pressure, but they should at least be polite. I trust they are well paid, so that cannot be the reason why they seem to resent answering the telephone. I suggest you invest in some retraining of your staff in how to deal with customers in a civil manner.

Secondly, they have on two occasions failed to listen to my instructions, with the result that I have incurred charges for services that I have not requested. I hope that under the circumstances you will refund the charges. If not, I must seriously think of transferring my account to another bank.

Yours faithfully

Roger Armitage

7 Aspen Street
Church Romford
Cheshire
WA45 5TY
29 June 20–

The Manager
Bank of the Northwest
Warrington
Cheshire
WA1 4RG

Dear Sir

I have recently started work in my first job. My employer wishes to pay my wages directly into a bank account, and at the moment I do not have one. Could you let me have some information on how to open a bank account, and tell me what the various types of account offer?

Thank you.

Yours faithfully

Jennifer Rowlings

4 Park Drive
Church Romford
Cheshire
WA45 5TY
5 April 20–

The Manager
Bank of the Northwest
Warrington
Cheshire
WA1 4RG

Dear Sir

Current Account No 45670199

I have recently retired and no longer need this current account.
Would you therefore arrange for the account to be closed and for the
existing balance to be paid into my savings account, No 44442311.
I enclose my current account chequebook.

Thank you.

Yours faithfully

Richard Kaczynski

5 Green Lane
Abingdon
Oxfordshire
AB3 5UN
11 July 20–

The Manager
Midlands Building Society
Upper High Road
Blandton
Oxfordshire
OX8 9AB

Dear Sir

Re: Mortgage Agreement 098/LBJ/85

I am writing to inform you that I am having difficulty in meeting my mortgage repayments.

My employers for the last 15 years, J M Smith and Company, went into liquidation in January and I was made redundant. I am actively seeking another position, but as you will appreciate employment is not easy to find in this area at present.

I have some savings in addition to my redundancy payment, but I am finding it hard to meet all my commitments. I therefore wonder if it might be possible for me to reduce my monthly payments by 20% and extend the term of the mortgage to allow for this.

I hope that you will give sympathetic consideration to my situation and agree to the temporary measures I have suggested.

I would, of course, be pleased to come and discuss this matter further with you, if you feel it would be helpful.

Yours faithfully

Malcolm James

It goes without saying that the first thing to do if you lose your debit card is to telephone the bank. Sending a letter will take at least 24 hours, during which time a criminal could be using your card to spend thousands of pounds.

51 Church Street
Royburn
Berkshire
RO3 9XD
11 May 20–

E. R. Cox
The Manager
London and District Bank
Amberley Drive
Royburn
Berkshire
RO1 2PK

Dear Mr Cox

Re: Account Number 0347599 – S. F. Dennis

I write to confirm my telephone call to your office this morning, in which I explained that I have lost my debit card.

I first noticed the loss yesterday evening. It may well be somewhere in the house, but I thought I should report it.

I last used the card on 8 May to pay for some goods at our local Co-op supermarket.

Yours sincerely

Simon Dennis

28 Bamburgh Crescent
Grimston
Suffolk
IP3 9XD
14 July 20–

The Manager
London and District Bank
Amberley Drive
Royburn
RO1 2PK

Dear Sir

Account No 34561289 Cheque No 424

To confirm my telephone call to your office this morning, the above cheque, dated 6 July and in favour of E. Taylor for the sum of £50, has apparently been lost in the post. Mr Taylor tells me he never received it. Please, therefore, put a stop on it and I will send Mr Taylor another cheque.

Yours faithfully

Roman Ungureanu

A telephone call is always advisable in the case of an overdrawn account. Banks like to be informed quickly and it may be possible to transfer funds into your account before it actually goes overdrawn. If this is unavoidable, you may need to negotiate an overdraft facility.

30 Eton Street
Hungerford
Berkshire
HG8 0EW
4 August 20–

The Manager
London and District Bank
Amberley Drive
Royburn
Berkshire
RO1 2PK

Dear Sir

Re: Account No 70790856, S. Black

It will have come to your attention that my account has been marginally overdrawn on four occasions in the last two months. I telephoned your branch this morning because I have bills for repairs to my car due to be paid soon, and I am afraid that this will happen again. The person I spoke to suggested that I write to you to arrange for me to have proper overdraft facilities up to £500. I will probably need this until the end of July next year, when my salary is due to increase and I will be able to repay the debt.

I would, of course, be happy to come in and discuss the matter with you, if you think that this is necessary.

Yours faithfully

Sylvia Black

White Gates
Bligh Hill
Haughton
Northumberland
NE46 6HJ
4 September 20–

The Manager
Bank of the Northwest
High Street
Haughton
Northumberland
NE46 4AA

Dear Sir/Madam

I have tried to use the cash machine outside your branch twice in the last couple of days, and it has failed to accept my card. I don't think there is anything wrong with the card because it worked in the machine belonging to the London and District Bank in Church Street.

I suggest you investigate whether there is something wrong with the mechanism in the machine.

Yours faithfully

William Perkins

15 Coopers Gate
Harmforth
North Yorkshire
YO14 5VB
4 May 20–

The Manager
Bank of the Northwest
23–25 Bank Street
York
YO1 4RG

Dear Sir or Madam

Account No 45623013

I recently received my monthly statement for the above account and
checked it through. I noticed two deductions, one on 2 April and the
other on 12 April, marked 'Administration Charges'. Can you
explain to me what these are for, please? As far as I am aware, I
should not have been charged for any extra services.

Yours faithfully

Millicent Strong (Mrs)

Credit

Obtaining credit is a big financial commitment and not one to be undertaken lightly. This is one area where it is perhaps best to look at all terms and conditions in writing – literally 'reading the small print' before signing on the dotted line.

Responding to a refusal to grant credit

20 Cedar Road
Hemel Hempstead
Hertfordshire
HH7 9BX
18 December 20–

The Manager
Maybrick Electrical
678 Pinder Street
London
W2A 4NM

Dear Sir

I am writing to ask why I have been refused credit by your company.

I came to your shop on 18 January to buy a washing machine and tumble dryer, at a total cost of £697. I understood from leaflets displayed in your store, and from advertisements in local newspapers, that you offer credit facilities to your customers and I therefore asked for the necessary paperwork to be prepared. I was most shocked when I was told the following week that this would not be possible in my case, a decision confirmed by the department manager, Mr Smith.

I would appreciate your explanation for this refusal, which has caused me considerable inconvenience and embarrassment.

Yours faithfully

Andrew Blackstock

There are three credit reference agencies in the UK. The following two letters are to a fictitious one.

20 Cedar Road
Hemel Hempstead
Hertfordshire
HH7 9BX
12 January 20–

Credit Search Ltd
130 Trentham Street
Manchester
M31 4ER

Dear Sirs

I recently suffered considerable embarrassment when I was refused credit by a high street retailer. I would like to know why and to ensure that it does not happen again in future, so I am writing to you asking if you could arrange a credit report for me. Please let me know what information you require from me and how much it will cost to prepare the report.

Yours faithfully

Andrew Blackstock

20 Cedar Road
Hemel Hempstead
Hertfordshire
HH7 9BX
3 February 20–

Credit Search Ltd
130 Trentham Street
Manchester
M31 4ER

Dear Sir

Thank you for the credit report.

I see now why I was refused credit in December by a high street retailer. There is a definite error in my credit history, because it is claimed by the London and District Bank that I defaulted on a loan that I took out with them. I do not understand this, because I am sure that I repaid the loan in full, and I am sure they would have chased it up if I had not. I have queried it with them, but they claim their records still show that I am in default.

I would be grateful if you could contact the bank on my behalf so that this dreadful error may be corrected.

Yours faithfully

Andrew Blackstock

Houses

Moving house is one of the most stressful life events. Putting all the fine details in a well-crafted letter could help ease the process.

32 Church Gardens
Dunham
Buckinghamshire
15 May 20–

Messrs Upley, Pope and Dykes, Solicitors
5–7 Broad Street
Dunham
Bucks
SB3 1BN

Dear Sirs

Re: 32 Church Gardens, Dunham, Bucks

This is to confirm our conversation of 14 May with Mrs Williams of your office, in which we agreed to your partnership handling the conveyancing arrangements for the sale of 32 Church Gardens and the purchase of New Farm, Chilton Maltravers, Bucks.

I understand that your estimated fee is £950.00, plus VAT, stamp duty, land registry fees and legal disbursement fees, and £500 for the home information pack.

The purchasers of 32 Church Gardens are:

Mr and Mrs S. Boyer
16 Berry Close
Dunham
Buckinghamshire
SB8 5SN

The vendors of New Farm are Mr and Mrs R. Chapman.

Please let me know if you require any further information.

Yours faithfully

Robin Austin

32 Church Gardens
Dunham
Buckinghamshire
15 May 20–

Robinson Whitlow, Estate Agents
19–21 High Street
Dunham
Buckinghamshire
SB6 1BD

For the attention of Miss Wicks

Dear Miss Wicks

Re: 32 Church Gardens, Dunham, Bucks

This is to confirm our agreement that your company will act as sole agents for the sale of the above property at a commission rate of 2% plus VAT. We understand that should we at any time decide to offer the house for sale through a joint agency, then the commission rate due to your company will be 3% plus VAT.

We also wish to confirm that the sales particulars you have supplied are satisfactory.

Yours sincerely

Robin Austin

32 Church Gardens
Dunham
Buckinghamshire
19 May 20—

Mr and Mrs S Boyer
16 Berry Close
Dunham
Buckinghamshire
SB8 5SN

Dear Mr and Mrs Boyer

Re: 32 Church Gardens

I understand from our solicitors that all the arrangements for the sale of the above property, and also for our purchase of New Farm, are proceeding satisfactorily. We expect exchange of contracts to take place at the beginning of August and completion at the end of the third week of August.

As agreed, I am listing here the items that we are selling as fixtures and fittings, but that do not form part of the main contract:

Brass door handles throughout

Carpets and underlay in all downstairs rooms and hall, landing and stairs

Slatted blinds on lounge patio doors

Lounge wall lights

Roller blinds in kitchen and bathroom

Bathroom wall cabinet

Curtains in master bedroom

Total price: £550.00

I would be grateful if you could send a cheque for this sum, made payable to R and J Austin, to our solicitors prior to completion.

Thank you.

Yours sincerely

Robin Austin

Insurance

It is fairly simple to compare insurance quotes via the internet, but if you don't want to fill out lengthy forms online, it is easy to collect information by letter.

To an insurance company asking for a quotation

14 Stoney Street
Wrexham
LL13 3GR
15 June 20–

Reliant Insurance Company Ltd
Pimlico Street
Aberystwyth
Ceredigion
Wales
SY24 1MP

Dear Sirs

My house and contents are currently insured by the Trustworthy Insurance Group and I am writing to you for a quotation for the same sums insured. I enclose a copy of the schedule and would be grateful if you could send me a quotation as soon as possible, together with any suggestions regarding improving my cover.

I would also like a quotation for motor insurance. I am 54 with a clean licence and full no claims discount. I am considering buying a new Vauxhall Astra 1.4GTi and would like comprehensive insurance for myself only. The car would be garaged at my house and only used for personal use.

Yours faithfully

Barry Spinks

It is very important to notify your insurance company by telephone as soon as possible after becoming aware of your loss. A letter may be sent as a follow-up.

29 Revell Road
Birmingham
B4 8BB
21 May 20–

Reliant Insurance Company Ltd
7 Browns Way
Birmingham
B1 2QQ

Dear Sirs

Re: Policy Number LN 985968

To confirm my telephone call to your office this morning, I wish to inform you that my home at the above address was burgled on the night of 19 May 20–.

Although my wife and I were in the house all evening, the theft was not discovered until 7.30 on the morning of 20 May, when we noticed that several items were missing and found that the kitchen window had been forced open. We immediately telephoned the police, who are now handling the investigation.

I look forward to receiving a claim form so that I can give you a full list of the missing items, with their replacement values. Please let me know if you require any further information.

Yours faithfully

Mohammed Hussein

25 St Andrews Court
Maidstone
Kent
MN6 9HD
15 July 20–

Trustworthy Life Assurance Co. Ltd
69 Croft Land
London
EC1 6DR

Dear Sirs

Re: Policy No 9469086

The holder of the above policy, Gerald Young, died on 28 June. I enclose a copy of the death certificate.

I am executor of his will. I would be grateful if you could inform me as to the amount of money the beneficiary will receive and on what date. Please confirm that the deceased's widow, Mrs Gloria Mary Young, is still the named beneficiary.

If you require further information or documents, please let me know.

Yours faithfully

Andrew Blake

Enc

Clubs and societies 7

Organising the activities of a club or society, however small, can be time-consuming and may require considerable diplomacy. The letters in this chapter are designed to help anyone involved in such a task. Also included are letters to the committee from ordinary existing or potential members.

General letters

Clubs and societies are often run by busy volunteers, who may well appreciate a letter that can be answered at a more convenient moment than an unexpected phone call can.

Asking for details of the club

15 Laurel Avenue
Bosfield
Dorset
BD45 1ER
15 March 20–

The Chairman
Bosfield Squash Club
Bosfield Common
Dorset
BD44 1SB

Dear Sir

I have recently moved to the village and am a keen squash player. I know few people in the village as yet, but clearly the squash club would be a good place to meet people, as well as to hone my game.

I understand that one sometimes has to be invited to join such a club, but as at present I do not know anybody who is a member, that poses some problems.

Could you let me know how I should go about applying to join?

Thank you

Yours faithfully

Anil Gupta

13 Tenby Road
Ronarth
Tenby
Pembrokeshire
TN23 4RO
12 February 20–

Dear Jim

I am writing to you to inform you of the formation of the Ronarth Local History Society, which I'm sure will interest you immensely in view of your great local knowledge. I remember talking to you about the possibility of forming such a society when we met at the Women's Institute dance last November. I recall that you indicated that you might be able to give some talks to the society on topics of historical interest, and I hope this is still the case. Even if not, we'd certainly like to invite you to join as a member.

The membership fee will be £10 per annum, and there will be a small charge at meetings when we have a visiting speaker and to contribute to costs for refreshments.

Our first meeting is an open meeting, and will take place on 4 March. I look forward to seeing you there.

Yours sincerely

Graham Selby

56 Spilman Drive
Longford
Berkshire
RG13 1UU
4 October 20–

Jim McBride
Group Scout Leader
1st Longford Scouts
Longford
Berkshire
RG13 4TQ

Dear Mr McBride

I understand the scouts are having a jumble sale in December, and I
wonder if there is anything I could do to help. My son is a scout and
no doubt you'll have plenty of help from the boys themselves, but
perhaps there is something that you would rather entrust to an adult. I
have quite a lot of experience of organising jumble sales and the like
for other village groups.

Please don't hesitate to ask.

Yours sincerely

Joan Sparkbrook (Mrs)

Offering to become a committee member

25 Ealing Road
Spole
Lincolnshire
LN12 4RT
1 November 20–

Mr Tom Wilson
Chairman
Four Winds Golf Club
Hatherway
Lincolnshire
LN17 1RY

Dear Tom

Now that Frank Armitage has moved away, leaving a vacancy on the
committee, I wonder if you would consider my offer to fill his place

until the elections in the spring. I feel that the committee needs to be at full strength to deal with all the demands of the growing membership, and my past experience on the committee of my previous club in Sussex would surely be valuable.

I realise that you may think my aim is to establish an advantage over other candidates in the election, but I assure you I only have the interests of the club at heart.

I look forward to hearing from you.

Yours sincerely

Patrick Brewer

Offering sponsorship

126 Prince Albert Avenue
Grizewold
Lancashire
PN45 7CV
3 June 20–

The President
Grizewold Rugby League Club
The Ground
Grizewold
Lancashire
PN78 6HU

Dear Sir

As you may know, I am currently a member of Grizewold Rugby League Club, although sadly my playing days are long over. However, I do like to support the club in any way I can, and I am interested in offering sponsorship to the club to help to encourage young players into the game. I would like to offer to buy a set of shirts for the under-8s team, which I would have printed with the club name and the name of my business, Acme Printers.

I hope you will be interested in taking up this offer, and I look forward to hearing from you or a representative of the squad.

Yours faithfully

James Cathcart

Meetings and events

Many people prefer written notice of dates, times and venues for events, so a letter would be appreciated.

Announcing a society meeting

Oakdene
Pershore Road
Stamford
Lincolnshire
SM2 5NV
12 January 20–

E. Turner Esq
17 Long Lane
Stamford
Lincolnshire
SM11 2XT

Dear Mr Turner

I wish to inform you that the next meeting of the Pershore-Stamford Debating Society will be held in the Parish Rooms on Thursday 26 November at 7.45pm.

Miss Rosemary Connors will open the meeting, supporting the motion 'That this Society views with alarm the increasing slide towards anarchy on our streets'. The opposer is Mr Keith Learoyd. The subject will be opened for debate when the speakers have concluded their presentations.

Yours sincerely

Stanley Archer

16 Blackford Road
Glasgow
G7 2RY
8 June 20–

Miss E Ward
19 Bearsden Avenue
Glasgow
G15 9MN

Dear Miss Ward

I wish to inform you that the annual meeting of the Blackford Operatic Society will be held on 30 July at Central Hall, Blackford Road, starting at 8pm.

Motions must be submitted in writing to me by 1 July if they are to be printed on the agenda.

The committee hope that it will be convenient for you to attend.

Yours sincerely

Agnes Hirchfield

Newton Prisoners' Friends Society
12 Fox Way
Newton
Tyne and Wear
NE56 4QM
Telephone 01234 567890
E-mail robert.farmer@usefulinternet.co.uk
5 June 20–

Dear Member

I am writing to everyone to remind you that our annual sponsored fancy dress chariot race will be taking place on Tuesday 5 August on the school playing fields. We need to raise as much money as possible through this event, so get together with friends to come up with some exciting and innovative ideas for chariots and costumes. Sponsorship forms are available from me. Drop me a line, give me a ring or e-mail me right now!

Best wishes

Robert Farmer

St Mary's School
Leaven Street
Stoke-on-Trent
Staffordshire
ST14 8RE
01135 999888
Email: exarts@StMarys.ac.uk
11 October 20–

News Desk
Post & Times
High Street
Stoke-on-Trent
Staffordshire
ST1 1PT

Dear Sirs

The Expressive Arts Department of St Mary's School will be presenting its version of 'Blood Brothers' in the school theatre 2–5 November, every evening at 7.30pm. At the final performance, a collection will be made and a raffle drawn to raise funds for the Children's Ward at Staffs General Hospital.

We should be grateful for any coverage of this event that your paper could give, as we are keen to promote not only our show, but also the fundraising for what I hope you will agree is an extremely worthwhile cause.

If you would like any further information or would like to come along to rehearsals to talk to some of the young people involved, please contact me.

Yours faithfully

Imelda Carter
Head, Expressive Arts Department

Llantoneg Rail Users Group
13 Chapel Close
Llantoneg
Gwent
NP44 3EE
12 November 20–

Dear John

As you know, the Superfast Train Company has just announced the closure of our station. This is a serious blow to the local economy, to commuters and to ordinary rail users. Superfast claims that the station is unviable, but we feel that this is a typical measure of privatised train companies, which put pure profit before service.

We are doing all we can to oppose the closure and as part of our campaign we are organising a protest rally outside the company's headquarters in Grandford on 10 December. I hope you and perhaps members of your family will be able to attend. We really need all the people we can get to make our presence felt.

We have arranged for coach travel to the event, but we may need to lay on extra coaches if the demand is there (I hope it is). So, could you let me know how many people there will be in your group?

Thank you.

Yours sincerely

Mike Armstrong
Secretary, Llantoneg Rail Users Group

16 Blackford Road
Glasgow
G7 2RY
14 October 20–

Mrs C. Armitage
34 Tremayne Close
Glasgow
G7 4GG

Dear Mrs Armitage

As you know, the autumn production by the Blackford Operatic Society was not a great success, and we made a significant loss for the first time in our history. This was a serious blow to the society and we are now somewhat in financial difficulties. We are considering a change in policy to stage shows in future that have more appeal to the general public. However, this depends on the society continuing to exist as a viable entity, and at the moment this is by no means certain.

I am writing to you as a long-standing member of the society to request a donation to our funds. Any amount you are able to send, however small, will be a help and I sincerely hope that it will be the last time that we have to make such a request. Once we are back on an even keel, I feel we can restore our reputation as one of the finest amateur operatic groups in the country.

Yours sincerely

Agnes Hirchfield

123 Adelaide Road
Chatsworth
Gloucestershire
CH5 2RG
16 July 20–

Alfred Thomas
Secretary
The United Rangers FC
Station Road
Porsham
Gloucester
G15 9YR

Dear Mr Thomas

We are currently drawing up our fixture list for the coming season and are keen to meet the United Rangers.

We usually have two teams, a First and a Second XI, playing every Saturday, one at home and the other away.

The dates that we still have vacant are:

List of dates

If any of these dates are convenient to your club, we'll be pleased to book them for both your First and Second XIs. We do not mind which team plays on your ground and which on ours.

Hoping that we shall be able to meet.

Yours sincerely

Roy Potter
Secretary, Chatsworth Rovers

Under the Elms
Porsham
Gloucester
G15 2RX
30 July 20–

Dear Roy

In reply to your request for a fixture with our club, I'd just like to let you know that Saturday 30 January would be ideal for us. If the kick-off could be at 2.15pm, that would be best. Would you like a return match at a later date?

If your First XI could play on our ground at King George V Playing Fields in Porsham, our Second XI will visit your ground. I hope these arrangements are suitable for you.

All the best

Alf (Thomas)
Secretary, The United Rangers FC

Committee matters

All committees are established and run under some form of rules and regulations. Having details in well-written letters can make record-keeping simpler.

Submitting a motion for an agenda

39 Atlantic Row
Glasgow
G7 2DS
10 June 20–

Mrs A. Hirchfield
16 Blackford Road
Glasgow
G7 2RY

Dear Mrs Hirchfield

I have today received your letter advising me that the annual meeting of the Blackford Operatic Society is to be held on 30 July.

I should like, please, to submit the following motion for inclusion on the agenda:

'That the society should cease to perform Gilbert and Sullivan and consider a range of more modern material, such as Rodgers and Hammerstein, in order to attract a younger membership and wider audience.'

Yours sincerely

F. K. Chesterfield

Bosfield Squash Club
Bosfield Common
Dorset
BD45 2AA
4 July 20–

Mr A. Gupta
15 Laurel Avenue
Bosfield
Dorset
BD45 1ER

Dear Mr Gupta

I have been asked to inform you that at a meeting of the Bosfield Squash Club, held in the club bar on 30 June, your name was submitted to the members.

I am pleased to report that you were unanimously elected a member of the club.

I enclose forms 3 and 4, which I would be pleased if you could complete and return to me at your convenience.

We look forward to welcoming you.

Yours sincerely

A. R. Bowley (Secretary)

The Castleways
Shirley upon Avon
Gloucestershire
ST4 9DB
1 April 20–

Miss N. Harket
Caversham Drive
Shirley upon Avon
Gloucestershire
ST9 2LU

Dear Madam

I have to inform you that the annual subscription of £20 to the Castleways Tennis Club is now due. Please send me your cheque before the end of this month.

Yours faithfully

Catherine Burke (Secretary)

The Three Turrets
Gemstone
Kent
BR9 2ZD
10 March 20–

Mrs R. Plunkett
The Old Rectory
Gemstone
Kent
BR5 4CH

Dear Madam

I regret to note that the annual subscriptions due to Gemstone Bridge Club from you and your husband are still outstanding. By the club's rules (No. 7), no member is allowed to attend meetings after 1 March if his or her subscription is still unpaid. In the circumstances, I should be glad if you could forward to me your cheque for £20 by return.

Yours faithfully

M. Jessop

20 Marchment Drive
Fishpool
Warwickshire
RG44 6VB
3 March 20–

The Managing Director
British Fish Products Limited
50 Derby Road
Stafford
ST1 6WP

Dear Sir

Fishpool Rovers FC

After the club's best ever season, during which we achieved promotion and a highly creditable 0-0 draw against Manchester United in the FA Cup, we are now seeking sponsorship for the coming season.

As you are no doubt aware, British Fish Products' distribution depot is situated just 100 yards from our ground, and we would be grateful for any sponsorship that you could offer. The benefit to you would be in excellent publicity, with the name of your company prominently displayed, and the opportunity to be associated with a progressive, successful football team.

In particular, we need sponsorship of our playing kit, which would mean British Fish Products' logo appearing on the shirts of our players, with an appropriate acknowledgement in the programme for each home match and advertisements for your products in the programme and around the ground.

Please let me know as soon as possible if you are able to provide this sponsorship. The new season is only three months away, and we need to move quickly to instruct our suppliers.

Yours faithfully

Alison Murray (Mrs)
Secretary, Fishpool Rovers FC

20 Marchment Drive
Fishpool
Warwickshire
RG44 6VB
3 March 20–

The Manager
Piper Electrical Store
High Street
Fishpool
Warwickshire

Dear Sir or Madam

Fishpool Rovers FC

After the club's best ever season, during which we achieved promotion and a highly creditable 0-0 draw against Manchester United in the FA Cup, we are now seeking help from local businesses for the coming season.

Any donation you could make, however small, would help us in bringing our ground up to the standard expected by the Football Association. In particular, our main stand is in urgent need of repair. The benefit to you of making a donation would be in excellent publicity, with the name of your company prominently displayed in the programme for each home game, and the opportunity to be associated with a progressive, successful football team.

Please send any donation to me, here at the club, making cheques payable to Fishpool Rovers FC.

Thank you.

Yours faithfully

Alison Murray (Mrs)
Secretary, Fishpool Rovers FC

Landlord and tenant | 8

Tenancy arrangements have to be clearly understood by both sides to avoid unpleasant encounters between landlord and tenant and the need for legal action. No arrangement can ever be perfect, but diplomatic language in letters can help overcome some difficulties.

Tenants

Having put all requests and questions in writing can help to protect your rights in the event of a dispute.

From a tenant asking for a reduction in rent

5 Antill Gardens
Brookhurst
Birmingham
B12 9XV
28 January 20–

S. Ladberry Esq
61 Turnfield Lane
Brookhurst
Birmingham
B12 7VG

Dear Mr Ladberry

I am writing to ask if you will agree to a reduction of the rent I am paying for the above address. I have lived here more than two years and during that time have not asked for an excessive amount of repairs, having done many small jobs myself.

I now find that I am paying more for this house than the sums paid by many of my neighbours whose houses are regularly maintained by their landlord.

I would be grateful if you would consider my request and let me have a reply as soon as possible.

Yours sincerely

S. A. Maidman

60 Waldemar Avenue
London
NW16 4JE
29 June 20–

G. A. Blay Esq
23 Highgrove Mansions
London
W3 4DX

Dear Mr Blay

I regret to inform you that yesterday the high winds damaged a number of tiles on the above property that I rent from you.

I would be glad if you could arrange for the roof to be repaired as soon as possible, since now when it rains, water comes in through one of the ceilings.

Yours sincerely

J. Sudbury

60 Waldemar Gardens
London
NW16 4JE
2 September 20–

G. A. Blay Esq
23 Highgrove Mansions
London
W3 4DX

Dear Mr Blay

I am enclosing the rent due for the above premises, for the quarter just ended.

I would like to draw your attention to the state of many of the rooms, which are greatly in need of renovation. The sitting room and the front bedroom are both very bad, with cracked plaster, and peeling paint and wallpaper. I would be grateful if you could attend to this matter as soon as possible. Thank you.

Yours sincerely

J. Sudbury

4 Seven Hills Road
Romley
Lincolnshire
LN30 1HJ
3 April 20—

Mrs J. Armstrong
2 Jam Factory Place
Romley
Lincolnshire
LN30 5ER

Dear Mrs Armstrong

I have recently received your letter informing me of a rent rise for the above property. I realise that prices have risen over the past year, but not by such a large amount as to justify such an increase. It is well above the rate of inflation, and I consider that you should reduce the increase at least by half.

I look forward to hearing from you.

Yours sincerely

Jan Mirsky

From a tenant threatening to leave if the rent is not reduced

4 Seven Hills Road
Romley
Lincolnshire
LN30 1HJ
23 April 20—

Mrs J. Armstrong
2 Jam Factory Place
Romley
Lincolnshire
LN30 5ER

Dear Mrs Armstrong

I am in receipt of your letter of 20 April in which you refuse to reduce the rent for this house.

I am sorry to say that, if this is your final decision, I shall be forced to seek accommodation elsewhere.

My wages have increased very little in the last few years and I know that there are houses nearby that suit my needs with lower rentals than yours.

I understand your position as well, but unless you can reconsider your decision, I will have to move.

Yours sincerely

J. Mirsky

From a tenant about overdue rent

3 Seacome Villas
Archery Fields
Arden
Suffolk
AN3 5FB
7 February 20–

M. Shawcross Esq
10 Alexander Road
Arden
AN10 2TP

Dear Mr Shawcross

I am sorry that you have had to write in connection with the rent, which is now overdue.

Unfortunately, at the moment I am unable to pay the arrears. The last few months have proved a great strain on my finances, largely because my wife has been ill and unable to work, thus reducing our normal income by about half. This is one of the drawbacks of freelance work.

Under the circumstances, can I ask you to wait a while longer for the rent? I will do my best to get the money together.

Yours sincerely

Peter A. Smithson

3 Seacome Villas
Arden
Suffolk
AN3 5FB
4 June 20–

M. Shawcross Esq
10 Alexander Road
Arden
Suffolk
AN10 2TP

Dear Mr Shawcross

I wonder how long it is since the central heating boiler in the flat was serviced. I have heard quite a lot on the radio recently about carbon monoxide poisoning from such boilers, and so I am concerned that this gas may be leaking into the flat.

Please could you arrange for it to be serviced as soon as possible.

Yours sincerely

Peter A. Smithson

Flat A
3 Main Road
Ryton
Cambridgeshire
CM12 2BB
7 September 20–

Environmental Health Department
Grandford City Council
Council Offices
Grandford
Cambridgeshire
CM34 1TB

Dear Sirs

I am writing to inform you that the flat I am living in is very damp and the heating has stopped working. I consider this to be a health risk. My landlord says he cannot do anything about it, so I am appealing to you to investigate. I understand that the landlord is legally responsible to ensure that such a situation does not arise, but I would like you to examine the property and tell me if I have a case.

I look forward to hearing from you.

Yours faithfully

Janice Costa

Asking for early release from a tenancy agreement

308 Cumberland Road
Manchester
MN25 4XP
21 January 20–

C. Potter Esq
24 Victoria Mansions
London
NW10 9DU

Dear Mr Potter

My husband has just accepted the management of a large plant near Bristol and we are anxious to move into that neighbourhood as soon as possible.

However, our lease of this house still has nine months to run. I would be grateful if you could let us know at your earliest convenience at what date and on what terms you would be prepared to release us from the remainder of our tenancy. We want, if possible, to get away by 1 May, and will, of course, be ready to meet any reasonable terms you may offer us.

Regretting very sincerely that we find it necessary to make this move, and with our kind regards,

Yours sincerely

Mary Brookfield (Mrs)

Flat 2
Holmedale Court
College Road
Blessop
Lancashire
UP8 4TC
29 August 20–

The Blessop Housing Advice Centre
Orion Precinct
Blessop
Lancashire
UP8 6TG

Dear Sirs

I would be grateful if you could advise me whether it is legal for my landlord to evict me despite the fact that I pay the rent regularly.

I have been renting a partly furnished two-bedroom flat at the above address for just over five years, during which time I have only once been in arrears with the rent. For the past year, the rent has been £325 per week and I have paid this sum to my landlord in person each week on time.

On 16 August, my landlord told me that he needed my flat for his brother-in-law's use. He gave me notice to leave by 15 September. I have told him that I cannot find alternative accommodation and that I will not leave. Yesterday he came to say that painters will be arriving on 6 September to redecorate the flat for the new occupant.

I cannot possibly find another suitable flat at such short notice and would therefore much appreciate your advice as to my legal position.

Yours faithfully

Stuart Hall

Landlords

The relationship between landlord and tenant is a formal arrangement that is best kept on a professional footing.

Reminder from a landlord to a tenant that the rent is due

6 High Street
Broadham
East Sussex
BN9 5HE
28 December 20–

R. Cuthbert Esq
2 Station Road
Broadham
East Sussex
BN3 4TP

Dear Mr Cuthbert

I have to remind you that the rent due from you on 25 December in respect of the premises situated at 54 Archway Street has not yet been received.

Please send me a cheque in settlement at your earliest convenience.

Yours sincerely

John Stewart

6 High Street
Broadham
East Sussex
BN9 5HE
1 February 20–

R. Cuthbert Esq
2 Station Road
Broadham
East Sussex
BN3 4TP

Dear Mr Cuthbert

The rent due from you for the quarter ending 25 December in respect of the premises occupied by you at 54 Archway Street has still not been received.

I regret to have to inform you that unless a settlement is forthcoming without any further delay, I will be compelled to take such steps as the law allows.

Yours sincerely

John Stewart

This letter should be sent by a signed-for delivery to ensure that the tenant receives it.

63 Woodhurst Drive
Poolford
Northampton
NN9 5TB
12 July 20–

Mr Peter Smith
94 Court Road
Poolford
Northampton
NN9 5TB

Dear Mr Smith

I have not received any rent from you since 30 March for the property that you rent at 94 Court Road. I am therefore forced to give you formal notice to leave. In accordance with your tenancy agreement with me, I am giving you four weeks' notice from the date of this letter.

Yours sincerely

Ian Graham

43 Singleton Mews
London
SW14 3DL
19 March 20–

G. Hunter Esq
27 Victoria Road
London
SW10 9XP

Dear Mr Hunter

I am in receipt of your letter of 8 March, and regret to have to inform you that it is impossible to consider any repairs to the house for some time to come.

During the last two years the major part of the rent has been absorbed by renovations and the property has been a severe drain on my own income. I consider the house to be in a habitable state, and while I do not wish to be unreasonable, I am unable to carry out any further repairs for the time being.

Yours sincerely

W. Smythe

43 Singleton Mews
London
SW14 3DL
19 January 20–

Miss Y. Khan
Flat 3
4 Armstrong Road
Brightend
London

Dear Miss Khan

I have arranged for repairs to take place at your property as requested from 15 February until 22 February inclusive. For this period, the flat will unfortunately be uninhabitable, and so I have to offer you temporary accommodation elsewhere. I have another furnished flat available at 50 Armitage Crescent for this week, and I would be grateful if you could examine it and see if it is suitable. If you call round at my house any morning between 10am and 12.30pm, I can let you have the key.

I hope these arrangements are convenient for you.

Yours sincerely

William Smythe

From a landlord refusing to reduce the rent

2 Jam Factory Place
Romley
Lincolnshire
LN30 5ER
20 April 20–

Mr J. Mirsky
4 Seven Hills Road
Romley
Lincolnshire
LN30 1HJ

Dear Mr Mirsky

I am sorry to say it is impossible to reduce the rent of the house of which you are the tenant.

When I originally fixed the rent I took into consideration that you were likely to be a good tenant, and set it at a low figure.

Were I to make a reduction, the rent you pay would barely cover repairs and the ground rent. I have really struggled to make ends meet over the last quarter, owing to my increased outgoings.

With regrets,

Yours sincerely

Joyce Armstrong

This letter must be sent by a signed-for delivery to ensure that the tenant receives it.

61 Turnfield Lane
Brookhurst
Essex
BK12 7VG
3 March 20–

G. Lauriman Esq
3 Denefield Cottages
Brookhurst
Essex
BK14 6HY

Dear Mr Lauriman

I am sending you formal notice that, as from 25 June 20–, your rent will be increased from £350 to £380 per week.

I am forced to take this step owing to the increase in the cost of maintenance of the property.

Yours sincerely

S. Ladberry

6 High Street
Broadham
East Sussex
BN3 2JK
1 February 20–

S. Davies Esq
3 The Terrace
Broadham
East Sussex
BN1 6NL

Dear Mr Davies

As your tenancy expires at the end of this quarter, I need to allow a prospective tenant to look over the house. Please could you therefore let me know when this would be convenient?

Naturally, the person in question would only come by appointment.

I would be most grateful if you could assist me in this matter.

Yours sincerely

John Stewart

58 Wexford Avenue
Beckenham
Kent
BK3 9EO
4 July 20–

C. Rose
The Parade
Beckenham
Kent
BK3 4XL

Dear Mr Rose

I acknowledge receipt of the statement of rents for my houses at numbers 2 and 5 Starwick Road, for the month of June 20–. I am glad to see that the tenants are paying regularly.

I note, however, that repairs are again required to the small bathroom at No 2. This is the third occasion in four months that such repairs have been necessary. I wonder if you could ascertain whether this is due to carelessness on the part of the tenants, or whether work done by the plumber you engaged is faulty in some way.

Please could you attend to this matter as quickly as possible, as I do not want any further repairs to be carried out on this bathroom until the cause of the problem has been established.

Yours sincerely

G. Talbot

Job applications and employment | 9

The letter you write to a prospective employer is absolutely crucial in establishing the quality of your application. Make sure your letter is well presented, includes all the necessary information and is precise and to the point.

Curriculum vitae

Most applications for a job require a curriculum vitae (CV) as well as an application letter, but do not send a CV on its own without a covering letter. Sometimes a prospective employer will send you an application form to fill in, which obviates the need for a CV. The object of the CV is to set out clearly details of your education, qualifications and employment to date. You should also provide personal details, including your name, address, telephone number and date of birth, and the names of two people who have agreed to act as referees.

Always be as brief as possible; a CV should not be an account of your life. Try to include only information that is relevant to your application. Ideally, you should be able to restrict the length of the CV to two A4 pieces of paper.

There are a number of ways you can lay out a CV and there are varying opinions about whether to start with your personal details and then go on to list your employment, or to do it the other way around. Choose the option that will give the most appropriate impression to the prospective employer. It is usual to list employment details in reverse date order so that your most recent (and probably most relevant) employment appears first.

The following are a few examples, but you are advised to refer as well to other publications more particularly focused on the subject of CV design.

You are not obliged to give your marital status or your age, and an employer is legally required not to consider this when recruiting.

Example of a CV of a school leaver without A-levels

Name:	Jane Brown
Address:	43 Chalcot Avenue London NW3 5DW
Home telephone:	0171 485 0387
E-mail address:	jbrown4562@hotmail.com
Date of birth:	22 August 1992
Marital status:	Single
Secondary education:	Chillingford Green School, Chillingford, London NW4 9DU
GCSEs passed:	English language (A*), Mathematics (A*), ICT (A), Geography (D), Textiles (B), French (A), German (B)
Employment:	Temporary clerical assistant at Jacksons Limited, Greys Road, Chillingford, NW4 0PT June–September 20–
Referees:	Stephen Taylor, Managing Director, Jacksons Limited, London Road, Chillingford NW4 9DU
	Mrs Mary Morgan, Head Teacher, Chillingford Green School, Chillingford NW4 0PT

Example of a CV of a graduate

Name:	Anish Kumar
Address:	43 Plunkett Road Coventry West Midlands CV4 8GH
Home telephone:	024 1234 5678
Date of birth:	8 August 1987
Secondary education:	2005–2008 Manchester University, BA (Second Class Honours) in History
	1998–2005 Streetley Grammar School, Coventry, West Midlands CV5 6YU
	12 GCSEs passed
	3 A-levels: History Grade B, Geography Grade C, Latin Grade C
Referees:	Mr K. Parks Department of History Manchester University M14 3DU
	Mr B. Crane, 23 Park Road, Coventry CV12 6TO

Name:	Elizabeth O'Grady
Address:	12 Newtown Road Fourways County Antrim BT40 5RR
Home telephone:	01234 567 890
Work:	01234 980 657
Date of birth:	9 August 1975
Education:	1987–1994 Kilfoyle Middle School, Linby Road, Fourways, County Antrim BT40 6TY GCSE passes in French, English Language, English Literature, Mathematics, Chemistry, Physics, History, Geography A Levels: French B English Literature B History B
Employment:	10 September 1994–30 October 1995 Insurance Underwriting Clerk at Trustworthy Insurance Company Ltd, 15 High Street Fourways County Antrim BT40 7UL
	2 November 1995–present Property Insurance Underwriter Reliant Insurance Company Ltd 100 Amber Road Long Armforth County Antrim BT50 3EW
Referees:	J. R. McClone Trustworthy Insurance Co. Ltd 15 High Street Fourways, County Antrim BT50 3EW
	Mrs M. R. Fisher, Reliant Insurance Co. Ltd, 100 Amber Road, Long Armforth, County Antrim BT40 7UL

Job applications

The quality of your letter to a prospective employer could make the difference between getting an interview and not, so take time to get it right.

Writing on spec to a potential employer

11 Main Road
Goodtrees
Nottinghamshire
NG50 3EW
4 June 20–

The Manager
Oak View Timber Merchants
40 Sherwood Way
Norton
Nottinghamshire
NG51 8YJ

Dear Sir

I have recently left Goodtrees Secondary School with eight GSCEs, including in Resistant Materials. I am writing to you to find out if you might have any vacancies now or in the near future.

I have very good manual skills and am skilled at using power tools. I know a lot about wood and the way to cut it, and I'm also very good with figures. One of my best results at GSCE was in Mathematics. Please let me know if you do have any vacancies. I live close by on the main bus route to your works.

Yours faithfully

Thomas Johnson

538 Pemberton Road
New Wood
London
N34 4WR
30 October 20–

The Chief Librarian
New Wood Library
New Wood Green
London
N33 5JK

Dear Madam

I am a student at New Wood School, currently in Year 10, and I am looking for work experience in a library. I would be very grateful if you could let me know whether this would be possible at New Wood Library. I am very interested in finding out more about how a library works, and having work experience there would be the ideal way to do this.

Thank you very much.

Yours faithfully

Sofia Beechcroft

Application for a job as a typist

38 West Park Terrace
Hamford
Dorset
DW15 5PU
3 September 20–

The Office Manager
Atlas Glassworks Ltd
15 Dean Street
Hamford
DW15 2XW

Dear Sir

I write in answer to your advertisement for a typist in this morning's Hamworth and District Advertiser.

I am 16 years of age and have just left St Veronica's School, Hamworth. I have GCSE passes in Mathematics, English Language, French, Art and Geography. I have good keyboard skills with a typing speed of 70 words per minute.

I would be pleased to attend for an interview at any time, and I am enclosing the names and addresses of two referees.

Yours faithfully

Susan Hellier (Miss)

Enc

Application for office junior post

89 Langley Avenue
Rangely
Hereford and Worcester
HR45 2QQ
23 August 20–

The Human Resources Manager
Trustworthy Insurance Company Limited
40 Market Street
Hereford
HR44 1TC

Dear Madam

I am responding to the advertisement in today's Guardian for a junior in your office.

I have just completed my education at Rangely School, where I passed 10 GCSEs, including English Language and Mathematics. I am a confident person and have already worked in one office on a temporary basis, and have learned skills such as answering the telephone that I feel would be useful in your office. I am well organised and feel that the type of work described in your advertisement would be ideal for me.

I enclose my curriculum vitae, which gives more information about my education and experience. My schoolteachers will be able to provide references.

Yours faithfully

Mary Biggs

77 Gerald Crescent
Somerleigh
Maidstone
Kent
MD13 2UQ
18 July 20–

The Personnel Manager
The Empire Trading Concern
10 High Street
Rotherham
South Yorkshire
RH10 9DN

Dear Sir

I wish to apply for the post advertised in today's Daily Telegraph.

I enclose a summary of my qualifications and experience, together
with the names of two referees. As you will see, I have worked in a
number of retail environments, and I already have experience of
selling electrical goods. I was a highly successful sales assistant at
Armstrong and Wise: I earned high levels of commission and was
recognised for my ability by being awarded bonuses. However, I felt
that the company offered little opportunity for personal advancement,
which is the reason I resigned, and I have worked freelance for six
months. In the meantime, I have been looking seriously for a new
post and the vacancy offered by your company seems to have
great potential.

I would be pleased to come for an interview at almost any time to
suit you.

Yours faithfully

G. Williams

Enc

Norfolk Lodge
Billington
Lincolnshire
LN7 9RS
6 May 20–

Dear Madam

Thank you for your reply to my advertisement for the position of a live-in nanny. In my present post, which I am leaving next month, I have had sole charge of four children since the birth of the youngest little girl, who is now five years old.

There are three other children: a boy aged six-and-a-half and twins, a boy and a girl, aged eight. As they are all now of school age, their mother, Lady Charles, has decided that she does not require a full-time nanny but intends to employ an au pair instead.

I am 32 years old and, as you can imagine, I am very fond of children, having worked with them throughout my career. My last post, where I stayed three years, was also as nanny to a family of four children, two boys and two girls.

I am presently paid £250 per week, with an allowance for expenses. Lady Charles has kindly offered to write a reference for me and I can provide others if you require them.

Please let me know as soon as possible if you wish to interview me, as I have had other answers to my advertisement.

Yours faithfully

Marion Russell

33 Ferndale Mansions
Southwell
Nottinghamshire
NG13 5RT
8 July 20–

Box 354
c/o The Daily Journal
Nottingham
NG1 1NG

Dear Sir

In answer to your advertisement in The Daily Journal of today's date, I wish to apply for the vacancy.

I am enclosing my CV, which gives details of my experience and qualifications. As you will see, I am well qualified to take up this post, and I would particularly like to draw your attention to my three years' experience at the RSPCA rescue centre.

I would be glad to come for an interview at any time that is convenient to you.

Yours faithfully

G. Gregory

Enc

Application for a job as sales representative

Hollydene
Collingwood Road
Norton
Lancashire
DH4 5UT
27 August 20–

Box 3998
The Daily Mercury
Lancaster
LA4 5PS

Dear Sirs

I would like to apply for the post advertised in this morning's Daily Mercury.

I worked for five years as a representative for Parkinsons' Pills, covering the West Midlands area, and I am at present working in Cumbria and Lancashire selling motor spares for Carparts Limited.

My weekly turnover at present averages £3,000.

I enclose my CV, giving full details of my qualifications and work record to date. I am 26 years of age and in good health.

Yours faithfully,

B. Gray

Enc

Application for a job as a store cashier

38 Fallowfield Road
Litchfield
North Yorkshire
NW30 2BQ
3 August 20–

The Manager
Stoker & Co. Ltd
Litchfield
North Yorkshire
NW29 8PS

Dear Sir

I wish to apply for the post of store cashier, which you are advertising as vacant in The Yorkshire Mail.

At present, I am cashier in the hardware department of Timsons' in Yarborough. I am 21 years of age and earning £360 per week. My reason for applying to you is that you are offering a higher wage and better prospects.

I am a quick and accurate worker and I have only had three days' absence in the last three and a half years.

I am available for interview at any time, but I need to give my supervisor a few days' notice if I am to take any time off. I am prepared for you to write to my present employers for a reference, but please do not do so until I have been for an interview.

Yours faithfully

Jane Jeavons (Miss)

Enc

13 Valley Road
Beechcroft
Surrey
MA67 8YH
3 October 20–

The Manager
Axford & Co. Ltd
Ramsbottom
Surrey
GU45 4TY

Dear Sir,

I am responding to your advertisement in The Independent this morning regarding your management training programme.

I have recently completed a history degree at West London University and gained a 2.1. I am aware that this is not a vocational course, but I consider the research disciplines acquired on the course to be highly applicable in the world of business.

I am an admirer of your products and have been for many years, and I would be very glad to be working in the environment in which they are produced.

I enclose my CV, which details my academic record and also gives information about the temporary work that I have undertaken.

I would be pleased to come for an interview whenever it is convenient to you.

Yours faithfully

R. G. Norman

167 Grove Avenue
Broomfields
York
YO6 4DL
19 November 20–

Roberts and Perry Ltd
23 Brighouse Drive
Birmingham
B14 9LD

Dear Sirs

Every week I have to call on 50 confectioners in the north of England and the borders region of Scotland. I am told that you have no representatives in this area. As your lines do not in any way compete with those that I currently promote, I could represent your goods to our mutual advantage.

Would you be interested in appointing me as your representative?

Yours faithfully

S. Cathcart

68 Middleford Road
Templeton
Gloucestershire
TE3 4DP
20 March 20–

G. A. Barrow Esq
The Tile and Timber Works
Templeton
Gloucestershire
TE1 5QR

Dear Mr Barrow

Thank you for your letter of 19 March in which you invite me to come for an interview for the post of site manager. I shall be pleased to attend, as requested, on Thursday 24 March at 3.15pm.

Yours sincerely

A. Pasquale

Accepting a job offer

51 St Paul's Road
Cardiff
CF4 8HY
18 October 20–

Mr R. Burns
Director, Human Resources
Timetec Ltd
Rose Estate
Oxridge
Buckinghamshire
SL9 5RF

Dear Mr Burns

Thank you for your letter of 12 October offering me the post of office administrator with your organisation. I am delighted to accept the position and look forward to starting work with you on 15 November.

Yours sincerely

Jane Allcock

Refusing a job offer

3 Streatley Road
Sydenham Rise
London
SE13 5RX
18 January 20–

George Barker Esq
The Towers
Beckenham
Kent
CB18 1TQ

Dear Sir

Thank you for offering me the post of chauffeur.

However, I was today offered a similar position at a higher wage. I feel it a duty to my family that I should accept the better wage, and I have done so. Therefore, it is with regret that I must withdraw my application to you, but I thank you, nonetheless.

Yours faithfully

James Hogg

Letters of reference

Even if someone has indicated that they will be a referee, it is a matter of courtesy to inform them that you have given their name to a potential employer. If you have not done so, and they receive a letter asking for a reference, they may not respond as positively.

Asking for a reference

48 Cambridge Road
High End
Lexford
Norfolk
LX14 9DB
4 September 20–

Dear Mr Browning

When I left school at the end of last term, you very kindly offered to be a referee for me when seeking a post. I am applying for the position of clerk in the Anglo-French Oil Company and have given your name as one of three referees.

I understand that the company may write to you and, if so, I hope you will be happy to write a favourable reference for me. The post is not a highly paid one, but it offers excellent prospects.

I would like to take this opportunity of thanking you for all you did for me while I was at school.

Yours sincerely

N. Scott

Brussington Hall
Northborough
Northamptonshire
NN5 6LU
8 May 20–

Dear Lady Charles

I am considering employing Marion Russell as nanny to my three children who are at present aged ten months, two and four years.

Miss Russell states that she has been in full charge of your children for five years and that they have been happy and healthy throughout that time. I would like to know whether you would agree with her on this and whether you consider her to be reliable and trustworthy.

Please could you provide any information you think may be useful to me in considering her for the post and let me know if you have any reservations about recommending her to me as nanny to my children.

Yours sincerely

Joan Foskett

Taking up a reference

The Loughton Works
Muchford
Hampshire
MC3 1FX
18 July 20–

Messrs Mayford & Co. Ltd
Portsmouth Way
Southampton
SO5 4DW

Dear Sirs

We have recently interviewed Mr Arthur Meyrick, who has applied for the post of cashier with us.

He has given your name as a referee, stating that he has worked for you for three years in a similar capacity. Please send us a note stating whether you consider him a suitable man to appoint. Any information you may be able to give us will be valued and treated in confidence.

Yours faithfully

G. R. Read (Director)

Mayford & Co. Ltd
Southampton
SO5 4DW
26 July 20–

G. R. Read Esq
The Loughton Works
Muchford
Hampshire
MC3 1FX

Dear Sir

Thank you for your letter of 18 July regarding the employment of Mr Arthur Meyrick.

My managing director has asked me to inform you that Mr Meyrick has indeed worked here as cashier for a period of three years. During this time he has proved himself to be efficient and capable, and his only reason for wishing to leave us is to seek a more remunerative post. Unfortunately, we are unable to pay him a higher salary, but this does not mean that we are in any way dissatisfied with his work.

If he is successful in his application to you, our company will be sorry to lose his services. At the same time, we would wish him well in his new position.

Yours faithfully

S. G. Smith (Personnel Manager)

Personal/character reference

These sorts of references are often given to school-leavers or graduates who have no employment history and therefore cannot call upon a previous employer for a reference. Some companies require a character reference in addition to references from former employers.

68 Middleford Road
Templeton
Gloucestershire
TE3 4DP
16 March 20–

G. A. Barrow Esq
The Tile and Timber Works
Templeton
Gloucestershire
TE1 5QR

Dear Sir

Thank you for your letter of 8 March in which you ask me to provide a character reference for my neighbour's son, James Reid.

I have known James since he was a child, and he has always seriously applied himself to his school work and this has paid off recently with some excellent exam results. He has a good circle of friends and is generally self-assured and outgoing. I would consider him to be reliable, straightforward and honest, and potentially very useful to you as an employee.

Yours faithfully

A. Page

Work-related issues

While day-to-day matters at work are usually best handled face to face, there are occasions when a letter is more appropriate, especially where the subject is of a delicate or personal nature.

Requesting change of hours

3 Bishop's Walk
Hampton
Suffolk
TW5 4XM
3 January 20–

John Harris
Manager
Part 2 Editorial
Hampton
Suffolk
TW5 8TQ

Dear John

As you know, my wife has recently taken up part-time work again after having the baby ten months ago. We agreed to split the child care up between us as best we could, with her sister stepping in occasionally if we were both occupied with work or other things. Unfortunately, her sister has had to go away for a while, and so there is about an hour each day late afternoon when we do not have any cover in the event of anything unexpected.

I am writing to you to ask if my shift could be delayed by two hours. I feel this should make no difference to my contribution to the output, and in fact it may be an advantage for me to finish two hours later to take care of some of the post-production issues.

I would be very grateful if this could be arranged, because we cannot afford to pay for child care.

Yours sincerely

Bob French

40 Church Close
Romford
South Humberside
DN39 3ER
4 April 20–

Arthur Edwards
Line Manager
Packing Department
Lister and Co. Ltd
Romford
South Humberside
DN39 9OK

Dear Arthur

I'm sorry to inform you that I'm going to have to take a couple more days off after my father-in-law's death. My wife has been particularly badly affected by this, because they were very close, and she needs me at home. Her brother will be over from South Africa on Thursday, and so he will be able to give her support then. The funeral is at the beginning of next week, so I'll need some more time off then, but hopefully that will be all.

I hope that's all right. I realise it's a busy time at work, but I haven't taken any holiday entitlement so far this year.

Yours sincerely

Sam Pickering

34 Trimble Rise
Carlisle
Cumbria
CA3 4HH
1 March 20–

Mr R. Preston
HR Manager
Ransome Pines
Carlisle
Cumbria
CA3 7FL

Dear Mr Preston

I telephoned your office this morning and spoke to Tracy Mardell. As I explained to her, I felt unwell and needed to go to the doctor.

The doctor has diagnosed tonsillitis, which surprised me because I thought that was something you left behind in childhood. He has given me the enclosed medical certificate for ten days off work.

Although I'm feeling rather below par, as you can imagine, if anybody in my department needs to know anything about the sales ledger, they can ring me at home. I hope I will be able to come back before the ten days are up, but I will keep you informed.

Yours sincerely

Ryan Mortimer

18 Hetherington Close
Birmingham
B2 7FG
21 January 20–

Mr M. Jones
Human Resources Director
Magitech Limited
Central Way
Birmingham
B1 1TJ

Dear Mr Jones

Thank you so much for taking the time to talk to me yesterday and for your kind suggestions to solve my present difficulties with my elderly mother and my children.

I now wish to confirm that I would be willing to try the flexible working arrangements that you offered. I understand that I would still have to be in the office for the core five hours, but being able to decide whether to start late and finish late some days would be a great help.

As I said to you, I have at home a computer with word processing software that is compatible with that used at Magitech. If there is an emergency at home and I have to leave early, I would be very happy to complete any unfinished work during the evenings or at weekends. Please confirm that this proposal meets with your approval.

Yours sincerely

Annette Hobbs

10 Vicarage Lane
Oxford
OX12 3RT
23 January 20–

Mrs Jane Haslam
Personnel Department
Technofit Ltd
Orchard Way
Premier Industrial Estate
Oxford
OX7 9KP

Dear Jane

I am writing to advise you of a series of incidents that have occurred at work over the past six months and that I consider constitute serious harassment, even bullying. This is obviously a very delicate matter and I have had to think very carefully before writing to you. But really the situation has become so bad that my health is suffering and I feel I may need to take time off work. In a way, this would represent a victory for the person causing me all the trouble, and also would give her the excuse to make matters even worse by saying that I am not up to the job.

As you may have guessed, the person at fault is my supervisor, Maureen Smith. When I first moved to the department, we got on quite well, but now for some reason she seems to dislike me intensely. At first the incidents were minor and amounted to silly practical jokes, which I took as such, but when she saw I was apparently not upset, this just seemed to annoy her. She then began trying to drive a wedge between me and the other girls, getting together with them and making fun of me. To their credit, some of the girls didn't go along with this, but there are a hard core who seem to want to do anything to please her.

The latest incident is more serious insofar as I have now been passed over for promotion because of Maureen's direct intervention. I have worked conscientiously, despite all the problems, and the manager had earmarked me for promotion, but Maureen advised him against it, telling what amount to lies about me to support her position.

This is a very upsetting situation, and I have had to write to you about it, because obviously my manager is more inclined to believe Maureen. I do hope you will be able to do something.

Yours sincerely

Sonia Gugelmann

10 Poplar Way
Ingleford
Hertfordshire
SG12 3RT
12 March 20–

Mr F. Brown
Human Resources
Baines Doors Ltd
Stevenage
Hertfordshire
SA17 9RE

Dear Mr Brown

I would like to take two weeks of my holiday entitlement for this year from 6 to 19 July inclusive and the other two weeks from 9 to 22 September inclusive.

I hope this will be convenient. Please confirm as soon as possible.

Yours sincerely

Alan Jones

27 Kinsbridge Mansions
Putney
London
SW15 9WW
28 October 20–

R. Fullerton Esq
Messrs Fullerton & Sons Ltd
Crawley Road
Sutton
SN3 5LW

Dear Mr Fullerton

I am writing to ask if you will consider an increase in my salary.

During the last two years I have not had an increase, though I think you will agree that many responsibilities have been added to my work during this period.

I am very happy in the office and like my work, but with the ever-increasing expenditure of a growing family, I find it difficult to balance my budget.

I should appreciate the opportunity to discuss this with you further.

Yours sincerely

G. S. Blackman

Such a letter is only suitable when the writer has some form of grievance against his or her employer and wishes to resign in a dignified manner. It is assumed that this grievance has been reported to the employer, but the employee is not satisfied with the response. Following this example is a letter when the parting is more amicable.

3 Ham Terrace
Hamborough
Lincolnshire
BS17 4EW
15 August 20–

Messrs Lindsey & Co. Ltd
Manton Way
Hamborough
Lincolnshire
BS17 3LC

Dear Sirs

I wish to offer my resignation, to take effect on 16 September 20–.

Yours faithfully

B. Mansbridge

This letter is suitable when the parting is more amicable.

3 Ham Terrace
Hamborough
Lincolnshire
LN4 7XG
15 August 20–

G. A. Lindsey Esq
Lindsey & Co. Ltd
Manton Way
Hamborough
Lincolnshire
BS17 3LC

Dear Mr Lindsey

I have recently accepted a post with Smith and Taylor Ltd of Merrowbridge and start work there early in October. I am therefore writing to give you the appropriate notice to terminate my employment with your company on 16 September.

I would like to take this opportunity of thanking you for all the support and guidance you have given me over the past five years.

I shall be sorry to leave the company but the new post carries with it greater responsibilities, and I feel that they will help to advance me in my career.

Yours sincerely

B. Mansbridge

Maternity matters

There is legislation in place to cover maternity leave, but nevertheless it is useful to put in writing anything relating to such matters, particularly if you work for an employer who has not had to deal with this topic before.

Asking about maternity leave entitlement

This is a letter to a Citizens Advice Bureau, which can give advice on all aspects of employment law. There is no question that the writer is entitled to maternity leave under the present law, but it will be useful for her to have all the facts to present to her employer.

45 Maple Road
Winton
Sheffield
South Yorkshire
S12 7VT
29 July 20–

Citizens Advice Bureau
17 High Street
Sheffield
South Yorkshire
S4 9TH

Dear Sirs

Re: Maternity Leave Regulations

I would like some information on the above. I am single, aged 30, and have worked for the last three years as a waitress at Corkers Wine Bar. I am three months pregnant but have not yet told my employer because I am afraid I shall lose my job.

Could you please let me know what protection I have under present regulations and what my maternity leave entitlement is?

I am sorry that I cannot call at your office in person because of the hours I work, but I would be grateful for any advice you may be able to give me.

Yours faithfully

Ann Blunt

26 Grant Road
Frinscombe
Essex
CH45 4RR
30 April 20–

Sally Marshall
Department Manager
Ladies' Fashions
Norbert and Peacock
High Street
Frinscombe
Essex
CH45 8BB

Dear Ms Marshall

As you know I am expecting a baby, and so I will be grateful if you can grant me the statutory maternity leave for the final stages of my pregnancy, the birth and looking after the child in the early weeks. I hope to be able to return to work but I have not yet decided for certain. I understand that you will be able to take on temporary staff to cover my absence during my maternity leave, and I trust that this will be satisfactory.

Although I am, of course, excited and delighted about the baby, I also feel a sense of responsibility towards the department, and hope that this will not cause too much disruption for you.

Yours sincerely

Lucinda Alcock

26 Grant Road
Frinscombe
Essex
CH45 4RR
30 May 20–

Sally Marshall
Department Manager
Ladies' Fashions
Norbert and Peacock
High Street
Frinscombe
Essex
CH45 8BB

Dear Ms Marshall

As I informed you in April, I need to take maternity leave in the next few months. If possible, I would like this to begin on 15 July, but some small adjustment either side of this date would be possible.

Please let me know if this is a convenient date.

Yours sincerely

Lucinda Alcock

26 Grant Road
Frinscombe
Essex
CH45 4RR
31 March 20–

Sally Marshall
Department Manager
Ladies' Fashions
Norbert and Peacock
High Street
Frinscombe
Essex
CH45 8BB

Dear Ms Marshall

As you know, I am intending to return to work soon and I wonder if it would be possible to adjust my working hours. I had been working five days a week, with Monday and Thursday off, but I should prefer to work for less time each day, six days a week. I have arranged child care, but working the long hours on the days I do work would mean I could spend very little time on those days with George.

Please let me know if you think we could come to a mutually satisfactory arrangement on this.

Yours sincerely

Lucinda Alcock

26 Grant Road
Frinscombe
Essex
CH45 4RR
14 October 20–

Ahmed Hassan
Department Manager
Men's Fashions
Norbert and Peacock
High Street
Frinscombe
Essex
CH45 8BB

Dear Mr Hassan

As you know, my wife recently had a baby, and the company allows me five days' paternity leave. At present, she is coping well at home because her mother is staying with us, so I would like to book the leave in a couple of months' time. I hope that will be convenient.

Yours sincerely

William Alcock

Business matters 10

The letters in this chapter cover a range of business circumstances and should prove particularly useful to people with small businesses or people who work from an office at home. These days it is very easy to create professional-looking stationery, and most word processing software programs enable you to design your own headed paper, with compliment slips, invoices and other paperwork all to match. Make sure that as well as your address, you include your phone numbers, and e-mail and website details, if appropriate.

General business letters

Many business letters are used repeatedly, so keep a master copy that can be adapted quickly and easily.

Acknowledgement

If you do not have time to deal with a matter straight away, it is better to write a quick acknowledgement so that the person sending the original letter knows that you have received it and are not ignoring it, which might be considered offensive.

Glaslyn
Cumberland Drive
Beckford
Shropshire
BD5 2JL
8 March 20–

Messrs Wilcox & Jones Ltd
21 Princes Street
Gloucester
G2 4RM

Dear Sirs

I acknowledge receipt of your letter of 4 March, which is receiving my attention.

I hope to give you a definite answer within the next week.

Yours faithfully

R. Goodyear

51 Goldheron Road
Shepherd's Bush
London
W14 0AD
6 May 20–

The Manager
Roberts Jewellers
9 Armstrong Road
West Kensington
London
W14 1JW

Dear Sir

I represent Satish Gold Rings and would like to visit you to show you some examples from our range. I could come to see you any day next week, beginning 12 May. Please let me know if that would be convenient, and the day and time that would be best for you.

I look forward to hearing from you.

Michael Kyriakedis

9 Armstrong Road
West Kensington
London
W14 1JW
10 May 20–

Mr M. Kyriakedis
51 Goldheron Road
Shepherd's Bush
London
W14 0AD

Dear Mr Kyriakedis

Just to confirm your appointment with us on 16 May at 2pm. We look forward to seeing you then.

Yours sincerely

George Brown
Manager, Roberts Jewellers

Apologising for not being able to keep a business appointment

51 Goldheron Road
Shepherd's Bush
London
W14 0AD
30 June 20–

B. Martin Esq
29 Shere Place
Reigate
RG4 2QN

Dear Sir

Since my letter to you of 24 June, circumstances have arisen that mean I shall be out of the country during the next ten days. I will therefore be unable to keep my appointment with you as arranged on 1 July.

I am sorry to postpone our meeting but after 10 July I shall be free to meet you at a date and time convenient to you.

Yours faithfully

M. Kyriakedis

Requesting information on a product

9 Armstrong Road
West Kensington
London
W14 1JW
11 June 20–

Mr M. Kyriakedis
51 Goldheron Road
Shepherd's Bush
London
W14 0AD

Dear Mr Kyriakedis

Thank you for presenting your range to us on 16 May, and I look forward to the delivery of our order.

I have a query on an item that you showed to us, which we decided at the time not to order. It is the sapphire ring with the snake design. We recently had an enquiry about such a ring, but the customer dislikes sapphires and we wonder if it comes with any other stone.

I would be grateful if you could let us know as soon as possible, because the gentleman concerned is one of our most valued customers.

Yours sincerely

George Brown
Manager, Roberts Jewellers

Enquiry about the price of goods

9 Armstrong Road
West Kensington
London
W14 1JW
17 June 20–

Mr M. Kyriakedis
51 Goldheron Road
Shepherd's Bush
London
W14 0AD

Dear Mr Kyriakedis

Thank you for the information about the gold snake-design ring, which you have advised us is available with a sapphire, an opal or an amethyst. Our customer is very interested in buying the ring with an amethyst, and I would be grateful if you could let me know your price for this item.

As before, please could you let me know as soon as possible because I am anxious to please this very loyal customer.

Yours sincerely

George Brown
Manager, Roberts Jewellers

68 Globe Villas
Wallerton
Salisbury
Wiltshire
S23 6VU
11 April 20–

G. Smithers Esq
18 Somerfield Drive
Salisbury
Wiltshire
S5 8JK

Dear Sir

A few days ago you were good enough to ask me to give you an estimate for certain repairs.

I have carefully checked over the work and now have pleasure in submitting the estimate. I may add that the figure quoted is for the best materials and workmanship.

Hoping that my quotation will prove acceptable,

Yours faithfully

N. Fitzwilliam

Enc

This letter could be sent to a batch of potential customers, hence its impersonal salutation and lack of recipient address.

15 Whitworth Avenue
Wrexham
LL13 3ER
30 June 20–

Dear Sir/Madam

I am writing to you to let you know about the new 'Splendid Vac 1000' vacuum cleaner, which is one of the most reasonably priced and powerful vacuum cleaners available. Based on a model previously only sold to businesses, such as hotels, offices and industrial premises, it has been completely redesigned and is now being sold to domestic customers for the first time.

I'm sure you will agree that this is excellent news, but you can't buy this outstanding machine in the shops. They are only being sold direct from the manufacturer to householders. As the appointed representative of Splendid Vac, I shall be visiting your area in early July, and would be pleased to demonstrate the 1000's amazing properties in your own home.

I enclose a brochure and a form for you to fill in if you wish me to call. I assure you, you won't be disappointed!

Yours faithfully

James Clinton
Splendid Vac representative

Orders and delivery

It is a good idea to confirm orders in writing, just in case goods or payment go astray.

Butler and Butler Ltd
91–93 Granby Road
Littleton
Hampshire
HA3 9XY
8 August 20–

Mrs B. Thomas
The Vicarage
Littleton
Hampshire
HA3 4PG

Dear Mrs Thomas

With reference to your letter of 12 July, and our reply, we regret to inform you that it will not be possible to supply the items you require within the time specified. We have now been informed by Coopers and Armitage, who used to make them in Surrey, that they are no longer produced in this country and have to be imported from abroad. Please accept our apologies for misinforming you.

Coopers and Armitage is reluctant to place an order for these items unless it is sure there is demand for them, so it remains unclear when they will next be available.

In the meantime we are enclosing some samples, which although not exactly the same as those you required, may be near enough to suit your needs. We can supply them at £30.58 each, plus VAT, and can deliver immediately.

Assuring you of our best attention,

Yours sincerely

James Butler
Managing Director
Butler and Butler Ltd

15 Whitworth Avenue
Wrexham
LL13 3ER
4 September 20–

Mrs R. Ainscough
River Cottage
Dell Lane
Wrexham
LL13 5NT

Dear Mrs Ainscough

I am delighted to confirm that your 'Splendid Vac 1000' vacuum cleaner will be delivered on Tuesday 14 September. I hope that is convenient for you. At present, I cannot give you an exact time, but if you would like to telephone the depot at 8am on the day, they will be able to give you a two-hour time slot. The telephone number is 0870 7123 4567.

I wish you many happy years of service from your 'Splendid Vac 1000' vacuum cleaner.

Yours sincerely

James Clinton
Splendid Vac representative

The Vicarage
Littleton
Hampshire
HA3 4PG
1 August 2008

Butler and Butler Ltd
91–93 Granby Road
Littleton
Hampshire
HA3 9XY

Dear Sirs

Order number BBL732/1

It is now three weeks since I placed the above order with you.

I should be obliged if you could let me know when I may expect delivery so that I can make space for the goods in my garage.

Yours faithfully

Mrs Brenda Thomas

Apologising to a customer for a delay in supplying goods

15 Whitworth Avenue
Wrexham
LL13 3ER
20 September 20–

Mrs R. Ainscough
River Cottage
Dell Lane
Wrexham
LL13 5NT

Dear Mrs Ainscough

I must apologise for the delay to the delivery of your 'Splendid Vac 1000' vacuum cleaner. Unfortunately there has been a hold-up in the despatch of the machines from Hungary, where they are made, to Splendid Vac's depot in Maidenhead.

I am told that this issue will be rectified in two weeks, at which time your order will be sent out to you. I will personally inform you when you can expect delivery, and hope that is convenient for you.

Once again, I must say how sorry I am that this has happened. As some compensation, I am arranging for you to receive a 'Splendid Vac' upholstery cleaning kit, worth £15.99, free of charge.

Yours sincerely

James Clinton
Splendid Vac representative

Accounts and payment

Anything relating to money is best confirmed in writing, particularly where there is some dispute about payment or terms.

Asking for a bill to be paid

37 West Street
Marlton
Buckinghamshire
SL7 2NB
15 September 20–

E. Wolverton Esq
3 Market Place
Billingsden
Buckinghamshire
BN2 5RT

Dear Sir

A statement of our account was forwarded to you on 10 August. We have not received a remittance, so it is possible our letter has been mislaid.

If this is the case, a copy of the statement of account is enclosed for your attention.

Yours faithfully

Frank Acton & Company

37 West Street
Marlton
Buckinghamshire
SL7 2NB
15 October 20–

E. Wolverton Esq
3 Market Place
Billingsden
Buckinghamshire
BN2 5RT

Dear Sir

We much regret that we need to draw your attention once more to the account forwarded to you on 10 August.

Payment is now four weeks overdue and we must ask that you make a settlement by return of post.

Yours faithfully

Frank Acton & Company

Threatening proceedings

50 Roman Terrace
Chalk Farm
London
NW1 9DP
16 July 20–

A. Campion Esq
2 High Street
Finchley
London
NW7 2PN

Dear Sir

I refer to my letters of 2 May and 8 June this year and wish to inform you that unless I receive payment for the antique pistols within the next seven days, I shall reluctantly have to place the matter in the hands of my solicitor.

Yours faithfully

F. Putnam

Eastwood Stores
High Street
Littlefield Green
Manchester
HG10 7NW
28th December 20–

M. Price Esq
17 Coronation Road
Littlefield Green
Manchester
HG10 5RZ

Dear Sir

We would be very grateful if you could send us a cheque for the goods supplied to you during October and November 20–.

Our accounts are balanced during the first week of January each year and the delay in receiving your settlement is preventing us from closing our books.

A duplicate invoice is enclosed.

Yours faithfully

S. F. Fothergill
Manager
The Eastwood Stores

Eastwood Stores
High Street
Littlefield Green
Manchester
HG10 7NW
15th January 20–

M. Price Esq
17 Coronation Road
Littlefield Green
Manchester
HG10 5RZ

Dear Sir

We regret to note that the account for goods supplied during October and November of last year is still outstanding.

We have already written to you several times regarding the matter and have sent duplicate invoices.

In the circumstances, we regret to have to inform you that, unless we receive a settlement in the next seven days, we shall be obliged to instruct our solicitors to institute proceedings against you.

Yours faithfully

S. F. Fothergill
Manager
Eastwood Stores

79 Redbridge Road
Burton Harcourt
Buckinghamshire
MK9 6DU
8 July 20–

S. Jefferson Esq
Burton Harcourt Motor Supplies
Burton Harcourt
Buckinghamshire
MK9 5RY

Dear Mr Jefferson

I am in receipt of your letter this morning with regard to our outstanding account, demanding payment by return.

I am sorry that the payment has been so much delayed, and I am as anxious as you to settle the account. Unfortunately I am unable to pay at the present time but I am confident that I shall be able to do so at the beginning of next month.

I sincerely hope that once the account has been settled we may continue to do business.

Yours sincerely

John Birch

79 Redbridge Road
Burton Harcourt
Buckinghamshire
MK9 6DU
15 July 20–

S. Jefferson Esq
Burton Harcourt Motor Supplies
Burton Harcourt
Buckinghamshire
MK9 5RY

Dear Mr Jefferson

I was surprised to receive this morning your letter threatening legal proceedings if I do not forward a full remittance within six days.

I deeply regret that you should consider such a step necessary. I have dealt with you for over two years, during which time I have always settled my monthly accounts very promptly.

Proceedings would put both of us to unnecessary trouble, without improving the position. As an old customer, I hope you will reconsider the matter, and allow me a little more time.

I am forwarding a small remittance on account, as evidence of my good faith, and would be pleased to discuss arrangements for payment of the balance.

Yours sincerely

John Birch

Alloa Road
Newington
Kent
NT2 4QR
11 August 20–

Messrs Perkins & Lambton Ltd
High Street
Newington
Kent
NT1 9PF

Dear Sirs

Please forward to me, at your earliest convenience, your statement of account up to and including 31 July 20–.

Yours faithfully

S. Warwick

1 Victory Lane
Twynham
Northumberland
TD14 9DR
15 May 20–

M. Taylor Esq
Twynham Garden Services
Orchard Hill
Twynham
Northumberland
TD14 6PN

Dear Mr Taylor

As you know, I am moving away from the district in a few weeks' time, so could you send your account to me, so that I can settle it before leaving?

I would like to thank you for the service you have given my family and myself, which I am sure will be sadly missed.

Yours sincerely

F. Carey

Alloa Road
Newington
Kent
NT2 4QR
15 August 20–

Messrs Perkins & Lambton Ltd
High Street
Newington
Kent
NT1 9PF

Dear Sirs

I have just received your statement dated 14 August 20–. Before settling, however, I need to draw your attention to the fact that item 4 does not agree with your quotation submitted to me on 6 July. Also, you have omitted to credit me with the value of the goods returned on 10 July, for which I hold your carrier's receipt.

When I have received an amended statement, I will forward to you my cheque in full settlement.

Yours faithfully

S. Warwick

Complaining of an overcharge in an invoice

168 Avenue Road
Highford
Powys
LD3 4DY
8 January 20–

Paul Jones & Co. Ltd
Station Road
Highford
Powys
LD3 9XY

Dear Sirs

I am in receipt of your invoice dated 1 January. As you will notice, the second item is for 15 reams of 80 g/m^2 paper at a cost of £6.25

each. These were sent with the original order, but were returned by me because I had not ordered them.

I am returning your invoice and, when it has been amended, I will be pleased to forward you my cheque.

Yours faithfully

R. Simpson

Asking for a cheque to be re-dated

Anglo-Australian Timbers Ltd
7 Forest Road
Pilton
Somerset
T53 6DU
8 July 20–

B. T. Fordham Esq
5 Cambridge Drive
Pilton
Somerset
T53 2DY

Dear Sir

We enclose a cheque for £15 that you sent to us six months ago. Unfortunately, it was mislaid until recently and now our bank will not accept it, as it is more than six months old.

In the circumstances we would be very much obliged if you could send us another cheque for the payment.

Yours faithfully

Brian Rodgers
Accounts Department
Anglo-Australian Timbers Ltd

Sample forms

In any business, it is likely that the same type of letter is sent out on a regular basis to different customers. In such cases, it is useful to have a standard form that can be personalised as required, as in the following examples.

Receipt
_____

75 Frith Road
Nottingham
NG8 7RH

Received from Richard Shipman, the sum of eight hundred and seventy-five pounds only, in payment for a Vauxhall van, registration number C365 NYO, delivered to him on 3 April 20–.

Brian Hicks

3 April 20–

Invoice

Pennine Motors Limited
Bowater Street
York
YO8 9TF
Vat Reg No 593 5739 27
19 November 20–

To:
A. P. Smith and Sons
49 London Road
Arbroath
AR9 7GD

Invoice No 76

Sale

Quantity	Description	Price, excluding VAT	VAT
1	Exhaust Pipe	£90.00	£15.75
2	Brackets	£25.00	£4.37
Subtotal		£115.00	£20.12
Total price			£135.12

Terms: 30 days net

Cash discount of 5% if paid within 14 days

Pennine Motors
Bowater Street
York
YO8 9TF
19 November 20–

Statement of Account

A. P. Smith and Sons
49 London Road
Arbroath
Angus
AR9 7GD

Date of sale	Reference	Amount
06.09.–	48200	CSH 29.75
16.10.–	48309	INV 43.96
21.10.–	48750	INV 8.44
23.10.–	48964	INV 18.94
Balance outstanding		£41.59

INV – invoice
CSH – payment received
CR – credit

E-mail | 11

What is e-mail?

The aim of this section is not to explain in detail what electronic mail, e-mail, actually is or how to get access to it. Nearly everyone who uses a computer will know this already, but not everyone is aware of the pitfalls that can occur, the limitations of the medium or the legal status of e-mail messages. There are times when e-mail can take the place of a letter, but times when it definitely cannot.

E-mail communication can be more akin to a conversation, if the two people involved are both working hard on their computers and picking up messages every few minutes. In such cases, the messages are usually very short and informal and so bear little resemblance to letters. But longer messages are often similar in structure to letters, even if the informality is retained. It is also possible to use e-mail for more formal letters in some circumstances, and to send documents, such as invoices, as attachments.

Think carefully before e-mailing

Perhaps the most important thing to do before e-mailing is to establish how often your intended recipient actually views his or her e-mails. Most people who use e-mail for business access their e-mails frequently, often setting their e-mail programs to download automatically, for example, every half an hour. But people using a computer at home may not do this, and could even go for days or weeks without checking to see if they have any e-mails. If this is the case, it is a poor method of communication and a letter would be more likely to be received and read within a day or two.

Even people who check their e-mails frequently do not always give them the same attention as they would a letter. They may receive dozens of e-mails a day, and they have to decide very quickly which of them are worth reading. Despite all the filters that exist on computer systems to keep out so-called spam e-mails, many still get through, and for some people these constitute the majority of the e-mails they receive.

There are inevitably occasions when it is difficult to judge from a subject line whether an e-mail is spam or a communication from a recognised source, and genuine e-mails can thus easily be deleted by accident. You are therefore advised to consider the subject line carefully, making sure it indicates clearly the content of your message. A letter, by contrast, has the advantage of being a physical entity, and is much more likely to be opened than a dubious-looking e-mail. After it is opened, even if the recipient regards it as junk mail, it still has more permanence than an e-mail, and a sales letter may still succeed in attracting somebody to a new product if it is left lying around on a desk.

Another drawback of e-mail communication is its propensity to be misunderstood. For example, it is often advised not to use humour in an e-mail, because the recipient may take the comment seriously, and probably be offended. A system of 'emoticons' has had to be created so that people can make their true meaning clear. These are arrangements of punctuation symbols that convey such notions as:

    happy :-)
    sad :-(
    confused {:%
    angry}:-*#

In some e-mail programs there is an option to paste into your message a little face symbol that provides the same information. (If the person receiving the e-mail does not have the same e-mail program, these images may not be received or they may be converted back to the arrangement of punctuation symbols.) It is beyond the scope of this book to describe emoticons in greater detail. They definitely have a use, but are despised by some people and are certainly inappropriate in business e-mails.

Exercise self-control

One consequence of e-mails being misinterpreted is that a recipient may be inclined to reply immediately and angrily. This is known as flaming and is best avoided. If the person who sent you the original message was not displeased with you and you send him or her an unjustifiably angry reply, you may lose a friend. Always take a disciplined approach when reading an e-mail. Read it more than once if there is something apparently offensive about it, and if you still think there is, query it with the sender. Not only do people misread e-mails, but they also mistype them and fail to check them before clicking on Send.

The immediacy of e-mail is an advantage over letter writing but it can so often cause problems. In writing a letter, you tend to think more carefully about what you are writing, and you also have some time, before you put it in the envelope and take it out to be posted, in which you can change your mind about sending it. Of course, you can also change your mind with an e-mail, but only if you have saved it to your Drafts folder before sending it. If you are planning to send a complaining or criticising e-mail, place it in your Drafts folder for a while and then come back to it in half an hour and reread it. You may find that your tone has been less than diplomatic and think it better to rewrite it. An alternative is to compose your rant in a word processing program first and save to your Documents folder, where you can edit it and then copy and paste it into an e-mail message if you decide to send it.

Dangers of forwarding

The ease of duplicating an e-mail, or part of an e-mail, also has its risks. Supposedly private declarations of love to an office colleague have ended up all round the office, and even on the other side of the world. The recipient proudly forwarded them to another colleague, who found them comical and saw them as a way of humiliating the sender, whom she regarded as the office creep. Always think carefully about forwarding any message or part of one, and, if necessary, get the permission of the originator. This is clearly another way of possibly losing friends!

The other side of the coin is that your comments about someone else may be inadvertently forwarded. For example, perhaps the recipient wants to quote your words on an important topic to someone else in a few months' time. He then searches back in his Inbox for your e-mail, block copies the section, and pastes it into his e-mail, quite forgetting the sarcastic remarks you made towards the end of the passage about your line manager.

Netiquette

Avoiding flaming and taking care when forwarding messages are part of e-mail etiquette, which when taken together with courteous behaviour in all forms of online communication – including forums, message boards, discussion lists, etc. – is often referred to as netiquette. Broadly, netiquette involves:

- *Being polite and respectful*, not only to the person you are writing to, but also about people you may mention in the e-mail. You never know who may read your message in future.

- *Avoiding 'shouting'*. The e-mail equivalent of shouting is writing in block capitals, and some people are inclined to do this because they think all the evidence suggests that the person they are dealing with is STUPID. But if you really want to get your point across, this is not the way to do it.

- *Avoiding offence*. Be careful not to write anything that may be construed by the person you are writing to as offensive to them, particularly because of their race, culture or sexual orientation.

- *Considering who else might be reading the message*, looking over your intended recipient's shoulder, or using the same computer on another occasion. For example, children have access to a family computer, so think about them when writing to one of their parents about an adult issue.

- *Avoiding jargon words or abbreviations*, unless you are absolutely sure the person you are writing to will understand them. Writing IMHO (in my humble opinion), HTH (hope that helps) or even LOL (laugh out loud) is liable to cause furrowed brows at the other end (although to be fair, it is always easy to find out what such abbreviations mean by looking on the internet), and you do not want to annoy your recipient by apparently writing in code.

- *Using correct grammar and spelling*. As stated earlier, it is easy to misinterpret e-mails, and grammar and spelling are important for conveying precise meaning. See page 259 for help on overcoming common pitfalls.

- *Thinking before using HTML.* HTML format enables you to use different fonts, colours, backgrounds and other features, but some e-mail programs cannot interpret this information and your message may therefore be illegible when it is received. This is not such a problem as it used to be because most e-mail programs can now cope with HTML, but if you have doubts, use plain text (the option to choose one or the other is usually in the Format drop-down menu).

- *Having an up-to-date virus checker.* If you do not, you can easily pass on a virus to another computer user in an e-mail. Even Apple computer users, who are rarely targeted by such criminal activity, can act as a conduit to pass on a virus to a PC user by receiving an infected attachment and then forwarding it.

E-mail as a substitute for a letter

Simply keeping in touch with friends is now more often done by telephone or e-mail than by letter. The main exception to this is when the friends live abroad, but e-mail is still a highly practical option in such cases. It costs very little and arrives with the recipient almost instantaneously (assuming he or she regularly checks for new messages). You can also send digital photographs as attachments, although this slows down the time it takes for the e-mail to send and be received, so make sure the files are not too large. Image editing software often has an option of saving a picture in a size suitable for e-mailing and e-mail programs also usually have some feature that gives you the option of limiting the size of image attachments.

The main advantage of a letter is its more personal nature. It is something that can be physically held and that bears the individual's own handwriting. It can also be kept and reread. The same can be said of e-mails, of course, if you haven't deleted them or you have printed them off, but they certainly do not have the same emotional quality. This can be very important for close personal relationships, such as those within families and between lovers. Thank-you letters may also be more appreciated by a recipient than if the thanks are sent electronically.

In general it is advisable to send a letter rather than an e-mail:

- If the content has some legal aspect or you are threatening to take legal action

- For job applications
- For official communications, such as complaints or objections
- For formal invitations

Letters generally carry more gravitas than e-mails, so if you are writing on an important subject, it is better not to use an e-mail. If making a complaint, for example, it is advisable to write, because it will be taken more seriously. In some cases, it may be useful to send both an e-mail and a letter, especially if you want to register the complaint as soon as possible. Put it briefly in the e-mail, and state that you will provide greater detail in the letter.

For anything that may have some legally binding nature, such as commercial agreements or contractual issues, a letter is almost always necessary. In some cases, electronically recorded signatures are acceptable, but usually a printed letter with a handwritten signature has more legal weight. If you are sending an invoice, it is better to attach a file created in a word processing or publishing program, complete with your business address, trade mark and/or logo if appropriate. This looks more professional than including the details in the body of the e-mail. However, be aware that if you send an attachment in, for example, Microsoft Word, it is possible for the recipient to change it using their own software.

Although job applications are also better sent by letter, sometimes prospective employers ask for applications by e-mail, and in such a case attach your CV as a separate document. If you are specifically instructed to submit your application by e-mail, resist the temptation to follow up with a letter and printed CV. Doing so is likely to cause confusion and even irritation, which will not help your prospects.

Subject line

It is impossible to send an e-mail without an address for the recipient, and your program will alert you to this omission; but it might not alert you if you forget the subject line. This can be crucial if you are trying to attract the attention of somebody who receives hundreds of e-mails in a day. So remember:

- *Make it relevant*, so that the person has some idea what you are writing about.
- *Make it short*. Lists of messages appear on screen in columns, and so ideally the subject line should fit in the column or part of it will not be visible. Column widths are up to the individual, so you

can never be sure exactly how long to make your subject line. Ideally keep it to five or six words.

- *If the subject has changed, change the subject line.* When using the Reply option, don't allow the program simply to insert Re: in front of the original subject line if you are now discussing something completely different.

The message itself

Although an e-mail message can be written in the same style as one you would use to write a letter, it is not usual to put the address at the top. Inserting the date is unnecessary, because the program will do that for you – unless your computer's date is set incorrectly, of course! The style is up to you, and depends on to whom you are writing. Many people avoid the normal salutation found in letters beginning with 'Dear' because they think e-mail should have a more informal quality. Hence, many e-mails begin with 'Hello' or 'Hi', possibly followed by the recipient's forename, or they just begin by writing the recipient's name. You may not be comfortable with this, and it does depend on how well you know the person, and the content of the message. If the e-mail is of a general nature to an organisation, there is probably no need to put any form of salutation. At the end, you write your name, or use an automatic signature (see page 254). E-mail's informal nature tends to mean that 'Yours sincerely' or 'Yours faithfully' are avoided in favour of something more friendly, such as 'Regards' or 'Best wishes', but, again, it depends on who the recipient is.

There are a few general rules regarding style in e-mail messages:

- *Keep it short.* Come to the point quickly, and don't go into too much detail. As stated earlier, attachments can be used to send more information. A major exception can be when e-mailing a close friend or relative, particularly when they live abroad. You may not communicate very often, but when you do, you want to send all your news.

- *Avoid fancy graphics and fonts.* These can be irritating and distract from any information that you want to convey (also, see the point about HTML on page 251).

- *Edit quotes from previous message.* When using the Reply option, the sender's message is usually quoted, which may be useful if you want to refer to it. But if there are number of messages on a topic passing between you, avoid quoting the entire correspondence so far in each message. This can make a message extremely long and is utterly pointless.

- *Show some respect.* Although e-mail is regarded as essentially informal, you still need to consider your recipient and it's usually best not to start by addressing someone simply with his or her forename. But this depends on the purpose of the message. Sometimes a very friendly approach is appropriate from the start.

The best advice is to use your common sense. If you are new to the medium, good e-mail style will come with time and you will soon learn which approach is best in each circumstance.

Signature

E-mail programs generally allow you to append an automatic signature to your message. This is a collection of information that can include your name, your position in a company, your business postal address, your home address, your telephone numbers(s), your e-mail address(es), your website address – anything you think could be useful in general to a recipient. You will find the Signature option in one of the drop-down menus. You can usually compose a range of signatures, and then use whichever is appropriate for your message, or none of them if you want to simply close by typing your name.

A word of warning: it's easy to forget about the signature and find that you have used the wrong one. Perhaps the default is a joking, fun sign-off that you normally send to friends, but if you include it in a message of complaint to your bank it is likely to undermine your position somewhat; but for such a serious matter you perhaps should have sent a conventional letter anyway.

General messages to several people

E-mail is ideal for sending a duplicate message to many people. Whether this is in the style of the general round-up letter often sent in Christmas cards (see page 38) or just some form of announcement you want to make to several people, e-mail programs make sending such messages very easy. There are a number of ways in which you can do this, and they vary slightly between programs. You can send the same e-mail to everyone in your computer's Address book, to everyone on a mailing list you have set up, or just to a few selected people whose e-mail addresses you paste into the To: field. Whatever method you choose, it certainly beats putting the same letter into lots of envelopes, addressing each one, buying stamps and posting them all!

A few examples of e-mail

If you have sought information about a company from its website, there is often a link that will allow you send a quick e-mail asking for further information. That saves you the trouble of having to find and type the address for the right contact.

From: tony.green@astralemail.co.uk

To: admin@choochoos.co.uk

Subject: Hornby Dublo tank engine

I have a Hornby Dublo 0-6-0 British Railways green tank engine from the early 1960s in excellent condition and I was wondering if anybody in your model railway club would like to have it. I'm not sure how much it is worth, but I'm sure we could find the going rate and agree a price.

Please let me know.

Tony Green

01234 567890

This is the same as the general Christmas message found on page 38, and you may feel it is still more sensible to print off a few copies and enclose them in Christmas cards rather than send e-mails – or, of course, you could always include a link to an e-Christmas card! However, if you think a general round-up letter is rather impersonal, sending an e-Christmas card is probably even worse in this respect. The following includes a signature at the end.

From: robertandjune@busybee.com

To: tony.green@astralemail.co.uk; jim@funmail.co.uk; rhunter@fastone.com; tracy34589@hotmail.com; rytonhome@busybee.com; ...

Hello, everybody.

It's been another very busy year for us, so we hope that you're not offended if we haven't been in touch. Hopefully, we'll put that right in the New Year.

Robert began a new job in March, and it's very satisfying. It's great for him to feel that he's actually making a difference. Fortunately, he's under less pressure to work long hours, which means he spends more time with the family. June is still busy at the shop and enjoys it immensely. Customers come from far and wide, and she often has people coming over 30 miles because they've heard from friends what a wonderful range of gifts she has. It's nice to be appreciated!

The children are still working hard at school, and we're generally very pleased with them and the school. Alice is coming up to GCSE and so is getting a little bit worked up about it. Fortunately, she has a good set of friends, who are all in the same boat of course, and they're very sensible about dividing time between work and play. John is as usual very sport-orientated, and has been particularly successful both in football and in cricket this year, with both teams trouncing the opposition in spectacular style. But he still devotes plenty of time to academic work.

We had a good holiday in Tunisia in the summer – a mix of lazing on the beach, seeing the sights, and desert trekking. In February, we're off skiing as usual, but a bit farther afield in the Canadian Rockies.

Hope you have a good Christmas and a Happy New Year.

Robert, June, Alice and John.

Robert and June Palmer
+44 (0)1234 567890
5 Lancashire Gardens
Hove
East Sussex
BN3 5TY

Informal business e-mail

To: apatel@junipermail.co.uk

From: rose.farmer@farinternet.com

Subject: Fibre-tip pens

Dear Abdul

Just to confirm our telephone conversation, we have a range of fine-point fibre-tip pens available in green, red, blue, and black, and could supply them at a cost of 12p each if you bought a thousand at a time. If you want to order today, just give me a call on 01234 567890 Ext. 4567, or you could visit our website www.fibre-tips-direct.co.uk.

Best wishes

Rose Farmer

Marketing Manager,
Fibre Tips Direct,
Malton,
Lancashire
PN45 5RT
Tel: 01234 567890 Ext. 4567

Some notes on grammar and spelling

12

Grammar is one of the building blocks of language, and language is essential for communication, so it follows that if you want to communicate effectively, you need to have some grasp of grammar. One problem many of us have is that we never really learned it properly at school. We learned grammar in French, German or possibly Latin, but we came to school as infants already speaking English, and it wasn't considered important to explain the difference between a subject and an object, or when to use 'that' and when 'which', never mind apparently obscure concepts like the subjunctive.

It is not essential that you get it right every time, and language is always changing, so some rules can be broken with no loss of understanding. The important thing is that you make your meaning clear, that there's no ambiguity, the things you want to stress are stressed and you hold the attention of your reader. Nobody likes having to decipher confusingly written text, having to draw on powers of intuition to arrive at some idea of what is meant. For one thing, if you send a letter like this, it can imply a lack of respect for the person to whom you are writing. If you can't be bothered to get it right, why should they bother to take any notice of what you are saying? On the other hand, if you break a few grammarian's rules but achieve your objective, then don't worry too much.

The word processing program that most people use, Microsoft Word, has a grammar checking facility. Unlike the spellcheck, it has very little value, and often queries things that are not mistakes. It is probably best to disable it, unless you wish to use it simply as a prompt.

Below are some basic rules and guidelines that will be helpful to anyone writing letters. Clearly, the more formal the letter, the more important they are. A few hints on spelling follow the grammar section below.

Parts of speech

This section is designed only to help you avoid common mistakes, and you don't need to know what all the parts of speech are called. But some explanation of what happens with verbs and nouns is probably necessary otherwise you may not understand what follows.

Verb

A verb used to be described at school as a 'doing word' and it essentially indicates an action being carried out, or a state of being. So *run, shout, lie, believe, exist, love, play, eat* are all verbs (although some can be nouns as well). If a sentence doesn't have a verb, it is not a sentence. The person or thing doing the action or being is the *subject*, and the person or thing that it is being done to (if any) is the *object*. So in the following example:

The boy kicked the football.

boy is the subject, *kicked* is the verb, *football* is the object.

Noun

Boy and *football* are also nouns, that is, names of things, animals or people. Words like *I, you, he, her, them, this, who* are pronouns because they are used in place of a name. Actual names for places, people, companies, organisations and institutions, such as *Edinburgh, France, Roger, Elizabeth, Dunlop* and *Aston Villa,* are called proper nouns and have initial capital letters.

Adjective

A noun can be modified by an *adjective*, a 'describing word', as in:

The red football

where *red* is the adjective.

Adverb

Adverbs modify verbs and adjectives. They often, but not always, end in 'ly', for example:

The wind blew strongly.

It was a bitterly cold day.

Be careful not to use an adjective (which adds to a noun) when you should use an adverb (which adds to a verb). The following example is incorrect:

You had better come quick.

It should be:

You had better come quickly.

Punctuation

These are the chief punctuation marks.

Full stop

A full stop is used at the end of a sentence or sometimes after a word that is abbreviated. Any letter following a full stop at the end of a sentence must be a capital letter starting a new sentence. Example:

I went to London yesterday.

Full stop at the end because the sentence is completed.

Jones and Co. is our company name.

Full stops at the end of the sentence and after Co. because it is an abbreviation.

Comma

The comma has very many uses, but its chief function is to divide up sentences into small portions so that the meaning is easier to understand. Using too many commas can destroy the flow of the sentence, so try to find the happy medium of having the minimum necessary to convey the sense. A comma before 'and' or 'or' at the end of a list of items is not the convention in British English but is rarely missed out in American English. Sometimes it may be desirable for the sake of clarity; this also may be the case before the conjunctions 'and' and 'but'. Examples:

James Prince of England arrived in Paris.

Without punctuation, the meaning of this sentence is ambiguous. Insert a comma after *Prince* and *England – James Prince, of England, arrived in Paris* – and the statement now clearly refers to someone with the name James Prince. However, if you insert a comma after *James* and after *England* – *James, Prince of England, arrived in Paris* – the statement now refers to a royal personage.

Typical high-street shops are Boots, Waterstones, Marks and Spencer, and BHS.

Here the comma after *Spencer* is to make it clearer that the *and* after *Marks* is part of the name.

Explanatory words or phrases, such as *however, nevertheless, in fact, consequently, therefore* and *indeed*, require a comma after them when they come at the beginning of a sentence, a comma both before and after when they are in the middle of a sentence, and a comma before when they come at the end of a sentence. Here are some examples:

She denied, however, having ever met the man.

However, she denied having ever met the man.

She denied having ever met the man, however.

The use of *however* to mean *but* in the middle of a sentence, even when preceded by a comma, is not correct. If you need to use *however* in this way, a new sentence is probably called for, or at least a semicolon.

Commas may also be used around phrases in a sentence. So, for example:

Felicity decided, despite not knowing a word of German, that she would holiday in Austria this year.

The phrase between the commas could be removed and the sentence would still make sense. This type of insertion of additional information is known as 'parenthesis' and the commas could be replaced by brackets or dashes.

Brackets

These are mostly used for the insertion of additional information in a sentence that usually qualifies or explains something in the main part of the sentence.

I wrote to Rachid (my brother-in-law, who is a solicitor) but he knew nothing about it.

Semicolon

A semicolon is often confused with a colon. A semicolon is a 'pause' halfway between a full stop and a comma and separates two distinct segments that are put together to form one statement, for example:

To err is human; to forgive, divine.

The pause provided by the semicolon adds more contrast and emphasis than would be suggested by a comma.

The part of a sentence after the semicolon may also be used to provide further information relating the first part:

The Socialist Party became the largest party in the upper house; it also held the balance of power in the lower house.

Another use for the semicolon is in separating the individual items in a list, particularly when the explanations of the items are long in themselves (and may already include commas). In such cases, the list is often introduced by a colon:

The house had a number of large rooms, including: a fully equipped kitchen, with two large ovens and a gas hob on the central island; a games room with snooker table, table tennis table and skittle alley; two bathrooms with Jacuzzis; and several bedrooms with en suite facilities.

Colon

The colon is used immediately before a list of things, as in:

The following words are nouns: boy, cat, dog, fish, men.

It may also be used as a link to more information that is signalled in the first part of the sentence, as in this example:

He showed them the real reason for his dismay: a stale Christmas pudding.

The way the first part of the sentence is worded leads you to expect an explanation.

Question mark

The use of the question mark is fairly straightforward. In a sentence on its own that poses a question, the question mark comes at the end in place of the full stop. However, if the question is only part of the sentence, then the situation may be different. Look at these examples:

Will you come to see me?

'Will you come to see me?' she asked.

In the first example, the sentence entirely forms the question and so there is no doubt over where to place the question mark. But in the second example, the question is only the part of the sentence that represents speech, and so the question mark belongs there, not at the end of the sentence.

In English, it is usually fairly clear when a sentence or part of a sentence is a question: the normal order of the subject and verb is reversed, as in the examples above, where *You will* has become *Will you*. This also happens in many other languages, but in some it is quite common for the verb and subject to keep the same order as they would have in a statement and for the sentence to be turned into a question simply by adding a question mark. When spoken, the normal raising of the voice at the end of the sentence to indicate a question also features in such cases. This does sometimes happen in English as well, as in:

You mean you don't want to go to the seaside?

A question mark is not correct when the question occurs in reported speech, that is, an indirect question. Look at the following examples:

He asked whether I was coming to the pub. instead of '*Are you coming to the pub?' he asked.*

She queried why the two figures were different. instead of '*Why is there a difference between the two figures?' she asked.*

Exclamation mark

An exclamation mark follows a word or phrase expressing strong emotion, such as:

Alas! The worst has happened, or *Long may he reign!*

It is also commonly used to indicate emphasis, exaggeration, amusement and sometimes even sarcasm:

You are too kind! or *This is just ridiculous!*

It is unlikely to be used in any formal letter. It is useful in e-mails to indicate when you are not being entirely serious; an alternative is to use an emoticon.

When an exclamation or question mark is used, it replaces a full stop or comma, so an exclamation or question mark and a full stop (or comma) are never placed side by side. Only use one exclamation mark at a time in formal writing.

Apostrophe

An apostrophe is used to indicate possession, as in:

the boy's book, the BBC's policy or *the soldiers' rifles*

The latter is plural, so the apostrophe is after the 's'. Be careful with plural nouns that do not end in an 's', like *children*, for which the possessive form is *children's* not *childrens'.*

An apostrophe is also used to show that something has been missed out, as in *back in '66* (meaning the year 1966) and verb contractions like *I'll* (I will), *isn't* (is not) and *don't* (do not). Contractions are generally to be avoided in a formal letter. A common mistake is to use the contraction for 'it is', *it's*, as a possessive, whereas *its* is correct. If you have trouble remembering which is which, think of the difference between *he's* (he is) and *his* (belonging to him).

Do not use an apostrophe in a plural. If you send a letter or e-mail to a potential client about the *conservatory's* you are selling, you are unlikely to sell one.

Just occasionally, some people will use an apostrophe in a plural to provide clarity, even though this is not strictly correct. For example:

When writing about individual letters – *minding one's p's and q's*

In the phrase *do's and don'ts*

Quotation marks

These can be single or double, depending on preference. Modern style tends to favour single over double. Quotation marks, sometimes called 'inverted commas' or (more informally) 'quotes', are used at the beginning and end of words, phrases or sentences that are actually said or quoted. But be careful not to do this for reported speech, which does not need quotation marks. For instance:

He said, 'I do not think it will rain.'

is a repetition of the very words the person used, so the quotation marks are required.

He said that he did not think it would rain,

on the other hand, does not have quotation marks because it is reported speech.

If you normally use single quotes, quotes within quotes will be double (and vice versa). For example:

He said, 'Do you know Paul McCartney's song "Yesterday"?'

Dash

Dashes and hyphens look similar but have rather different functions. A dash, called an en-rule by printers and word processing programs, is used in sentences to mark a break in the continuity of the reasoning. Example:

He brought the money – not that I asked for it.

Or it can be used to link words or names, or when you would say 'to' in a range

The 1970–74 Conservative government, the Rome–Berlin Axis, the Watson–Crick model

Dashes can also sometimes be used instead of commas or brackets as parenthesis in a sentence.

He wrote to Mr Forbes – who was at that time the chairman of the organisation – and told him that the true cost of such a plan would make it unattractive to the shareholders.

However, many people have a tendency to overdo this, which can make the reasoning hard to follow.

Hyphen
The hyphen, half the size of a dash, joins simple words together to make compound words. Examples:

day-to-day, tug-of-war, love-in-a-mist

It also features in double-barrelled surnames:

Mr Cholmondley-Warner

When to use capital letters
A capital letter should be used:

1   At the beginning of every sentence.
2   For the initial letter of every proper noun, such as a person's name, the name of a town, country, nation, etc.
3   For the initial letter of every proper adjective; in other words, adjectives made from proper nouns. Examples:
    The English people, the Indian mutiny, an American accent.
4   Whenever the personal pronoun *I* is written, no matter where it is placed in a sentence.
5   For the first letter of the days of the week *Sunday, Monday, Tuesday*, etc., months of the year, *January, February, March*, etc., and religious festivals such as *Easter, Christmas, Ramadan, Passover*, etc.
6   For the first letter of the names of the Deity, such as *God, Lord, Allah*, etc., and sometimes for the personal attributes of the Deity, or for pronouns used in place of the name, such as *His, Glory*, etc.

7 When a title is appended to the name, such as:

Queen Elizabeth II, the Duke of Marlborough, President Kennedy

But if the title is used on its own, there is generally no need for a capital (but neither is it wrong to use one):

The queen, the duke, the president

8 For significant events:

The First World War, the Wall Street Crash, the Reading Festival, the Lord Mayor's Show

9 The names of organisations, institutions, etc.:

The Houses of Parliament, the Confederation of British Industry, the University of Cambridge

10 For book titles, works of art, names of newspapers etc. In such cases, the minor words are usually not capitalised unless they come at the beginning of the title, for example:

The Grapes of Wrath, The Yeoman of the Guard, Arrangement in Grey and Black, The Daily Mail

Which and that

Strictly speaking, 'which' and 'that' are not interchangeable words; each has its own quite specific use, as outlined below. However, many writers use 'which' without ambiguity, and clarity is the most important thing.

'Which' is used generally to define further what has already been said:

The book on the table, which is mine, is by Charles Dickens.

Here, *which is mine*, tells us something more about *the book on the table*. 'Which' is always preceded by a comma, with another at the end of the clause. The implication is that there is only one book on the table and it happens to belong to me. The clause between the commas is almost incidental.

'That' is used when we want to indicate something. For example,

The book on the table that is mine is by Charles Dickens.

In this sentence, *that is mine* indicates that the book belongs to me. The implication is that there is more than one book on the table, and that 'my' book (to distinguish it from the rest) is the one by Charles Dickens. There is no comma before 'that'.

If you are unsure whether to use 'which' or 'that', read the sentence carefully and examine what it is trying to say. If you have used 'which' and think that the sentence would lose nothing if the clause within the commas were removed, you should probably use 'that'.

Ending a sentence with a preposition

Prepositions are words like *to*, *of*, *from*, *for*, and using one as the last word in a clause or sentence is generally regarded as a no-no for formal letters:

We have to decide what the new machine is going to be used for.

should quite properly be changed to:

We have to decide for what the new machine is going to be used.

but this sounds affected, so try:

We have to decide in what way the new machine is going to be used.

or perhaps:

We have to decide for what purpose you are going to use the new machine.

Different from, to, than

In British English, *different from* is generally preferred to *different to* or *different than*. In American English, the preference is for *different than*.

There's and there are

The use of the singular contraction *there's* (from *there is*) to mean the plural *there are* (for which no contraction exists) is becoming increasingly common in spoken English. For example:

There's two ways of looking at this

This might be acceptable in an informal letter, but it should be avoided in a formal letter.

Who and whom

Whom is the object case of *who* but it is widely ignored in spoken English in favour of using *who* all the time:

Who were you talking to? should really be *Whom were you talking to?* or more formally *To whom were you talking?* (to avoid the preposition at the end of the sentence – see above!).

This is the one rule of grammar that is also commonly broken in formal letters, and in fact using *whom* can sound rather pretentious, so in many instances it may be best *not* to use the correct form.

The split infinitive

Perhaps the most famous example of a split infinitive is the one that appears in the introduction to each episode of the *Star Trek* television series:

. . . to boldly go where no one has gone before.

The infinitive is the basic form of a verb, in this case 'to go'. In Latin, the infinitive is only one word, which obviously cannot be split, so 19th-century Classics scholars decided that an English infinitive should never be split by an adverb, in this case 'boldly'. Avoiding split infinitives has become generally accepted practice and they are still usually considered bad form, although to use one is not, in fact, a grammatical sin, as it is sometimes portrayed.

The most important thing for your writing is that it is not ambiguous or clumsy. You should aim for clarity of meaning and a smooth and flowing rhythm, so position your adverb accordingly. For example:

The director has promised to consider the project seriously.

is much better than both of the following options:

The director has promised seriously to consider the project.

The director has promised to seriously consider the project.

In addition to affecting the flow of the text, be aware that moving the adverb can change the meaning of a sentence, for example:

Our aim is to further cement trade relations with the European Union.

Our aim is further to cement trade relations with the European Union.

Our aim is to cement further trade relations with the European Union.

These three sentences mean different things. In the first, the aim is to consolidate existing trade relations; the second means that another aim (in addition to what has presumably already been mentioned) is to cement trade relations; and the third means that the aim is to achieve even more trade relations. If you wish to avoid splitting an infinitive, a more elegant solution might be:

Our aim is to cement trade relations further with the European Union.

Here is another example in which it would be ambiguous not to split the infinitive, as 'quickly' could then relate to 'learned' and not to 'play':

He learned to quickly play the piano.

not *He learned to play the piano quickly.*

This option is clumsy:

He learned quickly to play the piano.

Whereas this is both accurate and neat:

He quickly learned to play the piano.

Finally, be careful not to construct a complicated sentence to avoid splitting an infinitive when you would not really be doing so. For example:

The bridge is reported completely to have collapsed.

This sentence on the other hand is perfectly clear and correct:

The bridge is reported to have completely collapsed.

There is no split infinitive because *completely* does not come between *to* and *have*.

In general, the best outcome is usually achieved by focusing on clearly communicating your meaning without contorting your sentences.

Rules for spelling

There are hundreds of rules regarding the spelling of words in the English language, and a complete list of them would probably not be a help. It might even be confusing. So only the main rules are given here.

It is worth pointing out that Microsoft Word, the word processing program that most people use, has a very good spellcheck, but make sure you have it set for British English (and do read the cautionary verse on page 27). You can choose to have spelling mistakes identified as you type by a wavy red underline. It is also useful to help you spot where you have missed out a space between two words, for example. It will assume the two words together make one word, and in most cases that created word will not be a real word and so will be highlighted as a spelling mistake.

Another facility useful when correcting spelling mistakes is the Find and replace function. But be careful: avoid using Replace all, because you might change more than you mean to change. For example, if you decide you want to change all 'ize' endings on words like *organize* to 'ise', you could also change *size* to *sise* and *prize* to *prise* by accident!

Note: Apart from the vowels, a, e, i, o, u, all the other letters of the alphabet are referred to as consonants, even though 'y' can be used as a vowel substitute.

1   When a verb ends in 'y' and has a consonant preceding the 'y', and you want to change the tense or add a syllable to the word, change the 'y' into 'i' and add the syllable in question. Example:

Carry becomes *carried*, not *carryed*.

This rule does not apply when the added syllable begins with 'i'. Example:

Carry becomes *carrying*.

This rule only holds when the 'y' is preceded by a consonant. If a vowel comes immediately before the 'y', there is usually no change. But there are certain exceptions, which are mostly words of one syllable. The following, therefore, should be noted:

Pay becomes *paid*.

Lay becomes *laid*.

Say becomes *said*.

Repay becomes *repaid*.

2   When adding a syllable beginning with a vowel to a word that ends with an unsounded 'e', omit the 'e' and add the extra syllable. For example:

Move becomes *movable*, not *moveable* (although some dictionaries allow both spellings).

If the word ends with 'oe', do not omit the 'e', but retain it and add the extra syllable. For example:

Shoe becomes *shoeing*, not *shoing*.

If the word ends with 'ce' or 'ge', do not omit the 'e' when 'ous' or 'able' is to be added. For example:

Notice becomes *noticeable*

Peace becomes *peaceable*

Courage becomes *courageous*.

This is because the 'e' acts to soften the 'c' or 'g' and therefore cannot be missed out.

If, by omitting the 'e', the meaning of the word becomes possibly ambiguous, the 'e' should be retained. For example:

Singe becomes *singeing* and not *singing*, as this would be confused when written with *singing* (vocal).

If a word ends with 'ee' and the syllable that you wish to add begins with an 'e', one of the three 'e's must disappear. For example:

Agree becomes *agreed*, not *agreeed*.

3   The previous rule applies only when an added syllable commences with a vowel. If, however, the added syllable begins with a consonant, the final 'e' is retained. For example: *Peace* becomes *peaceful*, not *peacful*.

There are certain exceptions, however. For example:

Awe becomes *awful* (although *awesome* is correct)

Argue becomes *argument*

Due becomes *duly*

True becomes *truly*

Whole becomes *wholly*

4   One-syllable verbs and verbs accented on the final syllable that also end with a single vowel and a consonant double the last consonant when a suffix beginning with a vowel is added to them, as long as the emphasis remains on what was the final syllable.

For example, if 'ing' is to be added to the word *begin*, which ends with a vowel and a consonant, the consonant 'n' is doubled before the 'ing' is added. Here are some examples:

Begin becomes *beginning*

Beg becomes *beggar*

Glad becomes *gladden*

Confer becomes *conferred*

Rebel becomes *rebellion*

But:

Confer becomes *conference* with one 'r' because the stress is now on the first syllable

Similarly:

Prefer becomes *preference*

5   One rule we all remember from school (well, most of us anyway!): 'i' before 'e' except after 'c'. So:

believe, but *receive*

But a word of warning: you need to remember that this rule only really applies to words in which the 'ie' or 'ei' sounds like 'ee'. There are a number of other words, like *neighbour, rein, either, eight, height, heifer*, that are perfectly happy with 'e' before 'i' not after 'c'. A few to watch out for that don't obey the rule despite having the 'ee' sound are *caffeine, counterfeit, seize, weir* and *weird*.

6   In British English, there is a choice over whether to use *–ize* or *–ise* at the end of words like *organize/ise, authorize/ise, penalize/ise*. Some important exceptions are:

Exercise

Merchandise

Excise

Advise

These are always spelled with 'ise', even in American English.

One departure in American English that is not permitted in British English is the 'yze' on words like 'analyze' and 'paralyze'. Make sure you always spell them *analyse* and *paralyse*.

Plurals

1   The general rule for forming the plural of a noun is to add an 's' to the singular. For example:

Cat becomes *cats*

Dog becomes *dogs*

2   Nouns ending in 's', 'ss', 'sh', a soft 'ch', 'x' or 'z' form their plural by adding 'es' to the singular. For example:

Gas becomes *gases* (although *gasses* is also acceptable)

Lass becomes *lasses*

Thrush becomes *thrushes*

Church becomes *churches*

Box becomes *boxes*

Chintz becomes *chintzes*

If a noun ends with a hard 'ch', sounding like a 'k', rule 1 applies and an 's' is added. For example:

Monarch becomes *monarchs*

3   Nouns ending in 'f' or 'fe' form their plurals by changing the 'f' or 'fe' into 'ves'. For example:

Loaf becomes *loaves*

Life becomes *lives*

However, there are many exceptions to this rule, and the following should be remembered:

Chief becomes *chiefs*

Dwarf becomes *dwarfs* (except in Tolkien's *Lord of the Rings*)

Fife becomes *fifes*

Gulf becomes *gulfs*

Hoof can be either *hoofs* or *hooves*

Proof becomes *proofs*

Reef becomes *reefs*

Roof becomes *roofs*

Scarf can be either *scarfs* or *scarves*

4   Nouns ending in 'y' preceded by a consonant, change the 'y' into 'i' and add 'es'. For example:

Lady becomes *ladies*

If the 'y' is preceded by a vowel, Rule 1 applies and an 's' only is added. For example:

Boy becomes *boys*

5   Nouns ending in 'o' preceded by a consonant form their plurals by adding 'es'. For example:

Hero becomes *heroes*

Potato becomes *potatoes*

Tomato becomes *tomatoes*

But there are exceptions such as:

Piano becomes *pianos*

Portico becomes *porticos*

Proviso becomes *provisos*

Tyro becomes *tyros*

Fresco normally becomes *frescos* but *frescoes* is also acceptable

If the final 'o' is preceded by a vowel, the plural is formed in the normal way, by adding 's'. Thus:

Folio becomes *folios*

6   Some nouns have exceptional plurals. For example:

Ox becomes *oxen*

Mouse becomes *mice*

Child becomes *children*

Some nouns are the same in the plural as they are in the singular:

Deer remains *deer*

Fish remains *fish* (*fishes* is also possible, especially when referring to a small number)

Many nouns borrowed from other languages can follow the plural rules for those languages. For example:

Plateau (from French) becomes *plateaus* or *plateaux*

Stadium (from Latin) becomes *stadiums* or *stadia*

Proboscis (from Latin) becomes *proboscises* or *proboscides*

Appendix (from Latin) becomes *appendixes* or *appendices*

7   Compound nouns form their plurals by making the main word into the plural. For example:

Mousetrap becomes *mousetraps*

Mother-in-law becomes *mothers-in-law*

Passer-by becomes *passers-by*

8   Plurals are never created by inserting an apostrophe (see page 264).

Words that sound the same but mean different things

Some words in English that sound the same are spelled differently. Always check in a dictionary if you have any doubts, but here are a few common examples:

bite, *byte* (computing), *bight* (an indentation in shoreline, a bay)

cheque (payment from bank account), *check* (bring to a halt, examine)

seen (observed), *scene* (landscape)

hear (perceive sound), *here* (this place)

cents (currency), *scents* (perfumes)

feet (unit of measurement), *feat* (achievement)

ate (consumed), *eight* (number)

heir (successor), *air* (atmosphere)

wheel (thing that goes round), *we'll* (contraction of 'we will'), *weal* (mark on the body caused by a blow)

you (second person pronoun), *ewe* (female sheep)

isle (island), *aisle* (corridor between seats), *I'll* (contraction of 'I will')

ale (beer), *ail* (be ill)

new (unused), *knew* (had knowledge of)

not (indicating a negative), *knot* (join)

While the above may not cause many problems, the following two pairs certainly do:

your (possessive of 'you'), *you're* (contraction of 'you are')

their (possessive of 'they'), *there* (further away than here), *they're* (contraction of 'they are')

These examples illustrate the common mistakes:

Just e-mailing to find out if your *going to the match on Saturday.*

Bob and Sue came over on Sunday with there *two children.*

Words that often cause problems

Here are a few common examples of words that are frequently confused or misused. Sometimes this is because they sound the same or nearly the same as a word that means something else either very different or just subtly different. In other cases, frequent incorrect usage over the years has meant that often even educated people think they are getting it right, when in fact they are quite wrong. This is not an exhaustive list by any means, but it contains the ones likely to occur in everyday writing. If you need to know the difference between *ambiguous* and *ambivalent*, for example, you will need to look in a dictionary!

affect, effect

The common mistake here is to use *affect* instead of *effect*. *Affect* means 'to act upon, influence; to assume, pretend' and is not used as a noun. *Effect* is both a noun, meaning 'a result', and a verb, meaning 'to bring (something) about'. Here are some correct examples:

The minister's resignation did not affect the election victory.

She affected an air of superiority.

The storm had a devastating effect.

He effected change at the highest level in the organisation.

alternate, alternative

Both these should, strictly speaking, be used of two possibilities only. The adjective *alternate* means 'every other'; the verb means 'to vary repeatedly between two options':

We went to Birmingham on alternate Thursdays.

We alternated between the beach and pool for the whole week.

Alternative means 'something chosen instead of something else':

The sole was a very good alternative to plaice.

NOTE: American usage of *alternate* in some contexts to mean the same as *alternative* is rarely acceptable in British English.

among, between

When using a verb such as *share* or *divide*, *between* is only correct if two people or things are involved:

The books were shared out equally between the two girls.

For verbs such as *distribute*, when many people or things are involved, *among* is correct:

The food was distributed among the refugees.

breath, breathe

Breath is the noun (pronounced 'breth'), *breathe* is the verb:

He took a deep breath.

She could breathe more easily in the fresh air.

complimentary, complementary

Complimentary means 'giving praise, encouragement' as in:

Her excellent performance received many complimentary reviews.

Complementary means 'completing, filling in'. It's often seen in the term 'complementary medicine' used to mean acupuncture, homeopathy, osteopathy and other treatments that add something to conventional medicine but don't actually replace it. The term 'full complement' means 'the full number'.

comprise

This means 'to include, contain' and should not be used with 'of'. For example:

The house comprises a hall, reception room, dining room, kitchen, toilet with washbasin, two bedrooms and a bathroom.

continuous, continual

Continuous refers to an action that takes place over and over again without a break, whereas *continual* indicates something that happens a number of times but with breaks in between. *Continuous* is sometimes used when *continual* is meant, often implying a feat of endurance that would be impossible to achieve!

dessert, desert

The first is the pudding, the second the hot, sandy, desolate region. The double 's' in the first may be surprising, because the pronunciation makes it sound like there should be only one 's'. (*Desert* with one 's' is also the spelling for the word meaning 'to abandon', although the stress is on the second syllable.)

fewer, less

A very common mistake in spoken English is to use less when fewer would be correct. Less should only be used with nouns when indicating quantity, for example:

less time; less money; less water; less sleep

When you are referring to numbers of things or people, *fewer* is needed:

Fewer people; there were fewer than forty left

Unfortunately, it gets complicated in phrases like:

Less than eight

which can be right in the sentence:

Is the number seven more than or less than eight?

I waited for less than 30 minutes

is also correct, because the 30 minutes is predominantly a notion of quantity.

flounder, founder

Flounder means 'to struggle, move with difficulty' but is often mistakenly used instead of *founder*, which means 'to sink, fail', as in:

The ship foundered on the rocks and the passengers had to take to the lifeboats.

historic, historical

Generally speaking, *historic* refers to major, ground-breaking events, like landing on the Moon, whereas *historical* means 'relating to history', as in the phrase 'a historical novel'. However, clearly in some circumstances both could be correct: the Moon landing was a historic event insofar as no one had done it before, but it is also now a historical event, something that happened in July 1969. Historic is also used to describe a place that has a lot of history associated with it, like 'historic York'.

Incidentally, it is sometimes thought to be correct to use 'an' before these two words, rather than 'a', but there is really no good reason for this. The 'h' is a consonant and is sounded, so 'a' is correct (whereas 'an' is correct before *honest*, for example, because its 'h' is unsounded), but because 'an' is used so much by so many people, there is perhaps a case for regarding it as acceptable. Perhaps there are historical reasons for this…

infer, imply

The original – and for many people, the only correct – definition of *infer* is 'to draw conclusions from, to deduce', while *imply* means to 'suggest or indicate'. However, the difference has become blurred by common usage to the extent that some newer dictionaries have accepted that *infer* can also be used to mean the same as *imply*.

insure, ensure

Insure means 'to protect against financial risk', in other words, to take out an insurance policy, whereas *ensure* means 'to make certain'. (Something that is *assured* is bound to happen, which is why we have home insurance but life assurance policies.)

liquor, liqueur

The first (pronounced 'licker') can refer to alcoholic drink in general, particular strong alcohol, whereas the second (pronounced 'li-cure') means a highly flavoured sweetened spirit such as Cointreau or Drambuie.

loath, loathe

Loath (sometimes *loth*) means 'reluctant, unwilling' as in:

He was loath to admit his mistake.

Loathe means 'to dislike, hate':

He loathed his mother-in-law.

loose, lose

Loose is the opposite of 'tight', and can also mean 'to let go'. *Lose* is 'to misplace'.

moral, morale

Moral means 'ethical', as in this example:

He was a very moral man and never avoided paying his taxes.

As a noun, it means a lesson or example provided by a story:

The moral of the tale is that you should always look before you leap.

Morale, on the other hand, means 'spirit, self-confidence':

The troops' morale remained high despite the defeat.

phase, faze

These two sound exactly the same, but the first means 'a stage in a process' whereas the second means 'to worry, disconcert':

We are now approaching the second phase in the building work.

He was not fazed by the howling of the wolves.

perverse, perverted

Perverse means 'wayward, awkward, obstinate' and is not as strong as *perverted*, which means 'deviant, corrupt'. There is a danger of *perverse*, a fairly mild criticism, being misinterpreted as something a lot more serious.

tortuous

This means 'twisting, winding; devious' and has nothing at all to do with torture.

uninterested, disinterested

Uninterested means not being interested, whereas *disinterested* means being impartial. UN observers of elections in countries can provide an assessment of the fairness of those elections because they are *disinterested*, but that does not mean they don't find the elections interesting.

Some words that are often misspelled

accommodation
across
address
Arctic and *Antarctic*
bazaar
benefited, benefiting
bizarre
broccoli
caffeine
catarrh
catastrophe
commemorate
comparative
conscience
conscientious
counterfeit
crystal
defence, but *defensive*
diarrhoea
embarrass
endeavour
enrol, enrolment
environment
excellent
excite
exercise
extraordinary
favourite (the American spelling *favorite* is often used on computers)
forfeit
forty
fulfil
gauge
government
handkerchief
humour, but *humorous*
hygiene
indelible
innocent
innocuous

inoculate
interrupt
jeopardy
jewellery
licence (noun)
license (verb),
lieutenant (pronounced 'lef-tenant' in Britain, 'loo-tenant' in the US)
manoeuvre
margarine
marvel, marvellous
Mediterranean
millennium
minuscule
Morocco
ninth
ninety
overreact
parliament
phenomena (plural of *phenomenon* but often mistakenly used as a singular)
Philippines
possessive, possession
practice (noun)
practise (verb)
precede
privilege
proceed
pronunciation
questionnaire
raspberry
recommend
rhyme
rhythm
seize
subtly
supersede
targeted, targeting
threshold
tranquillity
travelling
under way (two words)

weir
weird
wilful
woollen

If in doubt, check it out

It will be clear from the above that English spelling and grammar are full of inconsistencies and that there are many exceptions to the so-called rules. If you have any doubts, check in a dictionary or a reference work such as *Fowler's Modern English Usage*. You will find *Really Simple English Grammar* (Foulsham, 978-0-572-02811-4) a simple and practical guide to improving your written English.

Index